ISBN-13: 978-1542513517
ISBN-10: 1542513510

FACES OF CULTURE

Skye Wright

Dedicated to all those grown ups who still love to color.
May your inner child shine bright.

&

To my family and friends...
You make my world go round.

About the Author

Skye Wright has had a love affair with art since early childhood. Self taught, she learned through trial and error, study and practice, patience and persistence. As an adult she added in an eclectic education of work, travel and college to make her the artist she is today.

Inspired by the vast and unique artistic expressions of individuals that she has seen through her own personal study and travels. The artist here has captured the raw and simple beauty that makes each person unique to there own tribe, people and nation. Each face presented here is meant to celebrate the beauty and diversity that makes this world so interesting to live in and be a part of.

What makes you and me wonderful are the things that set us apart.

www.skyewright.com

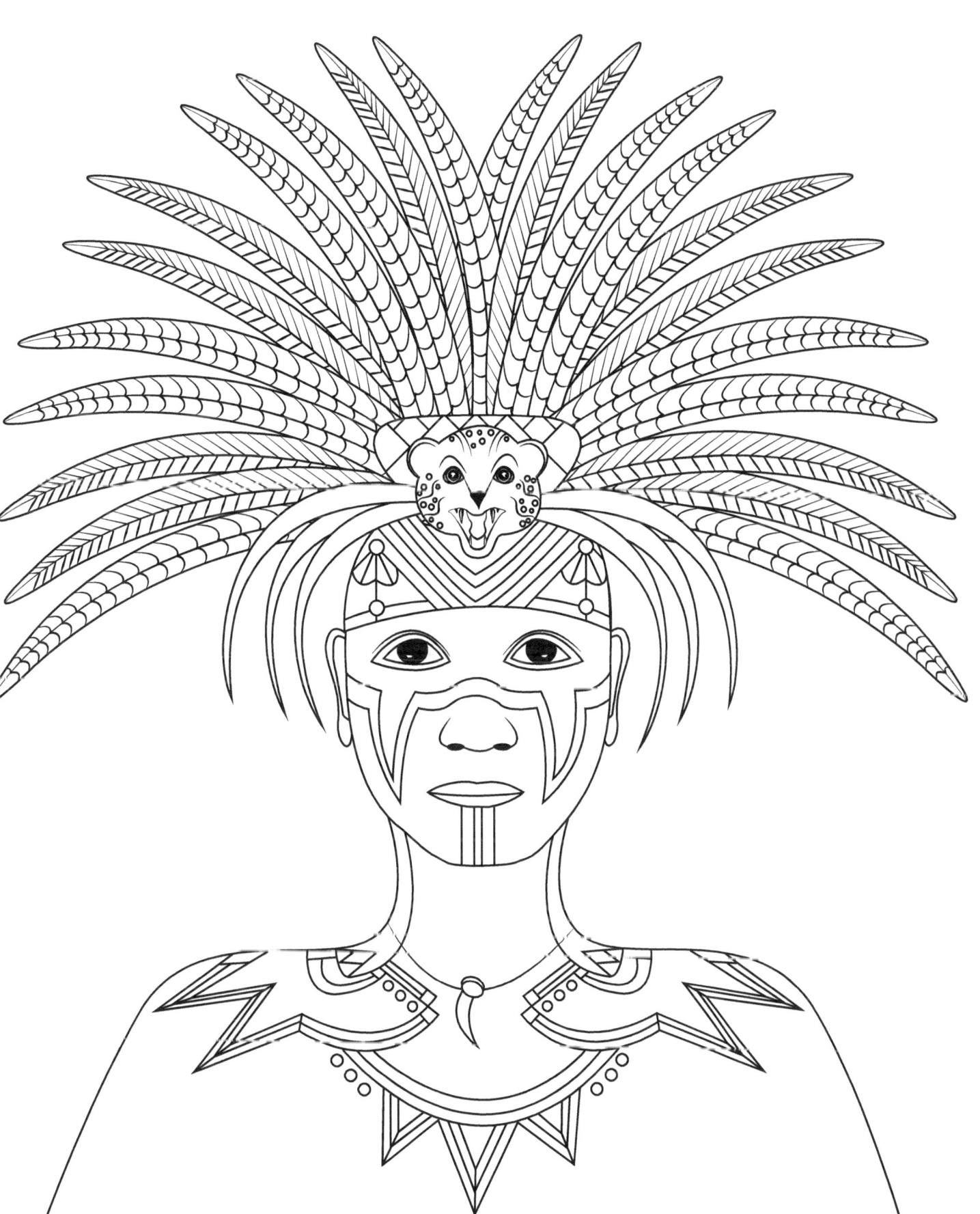

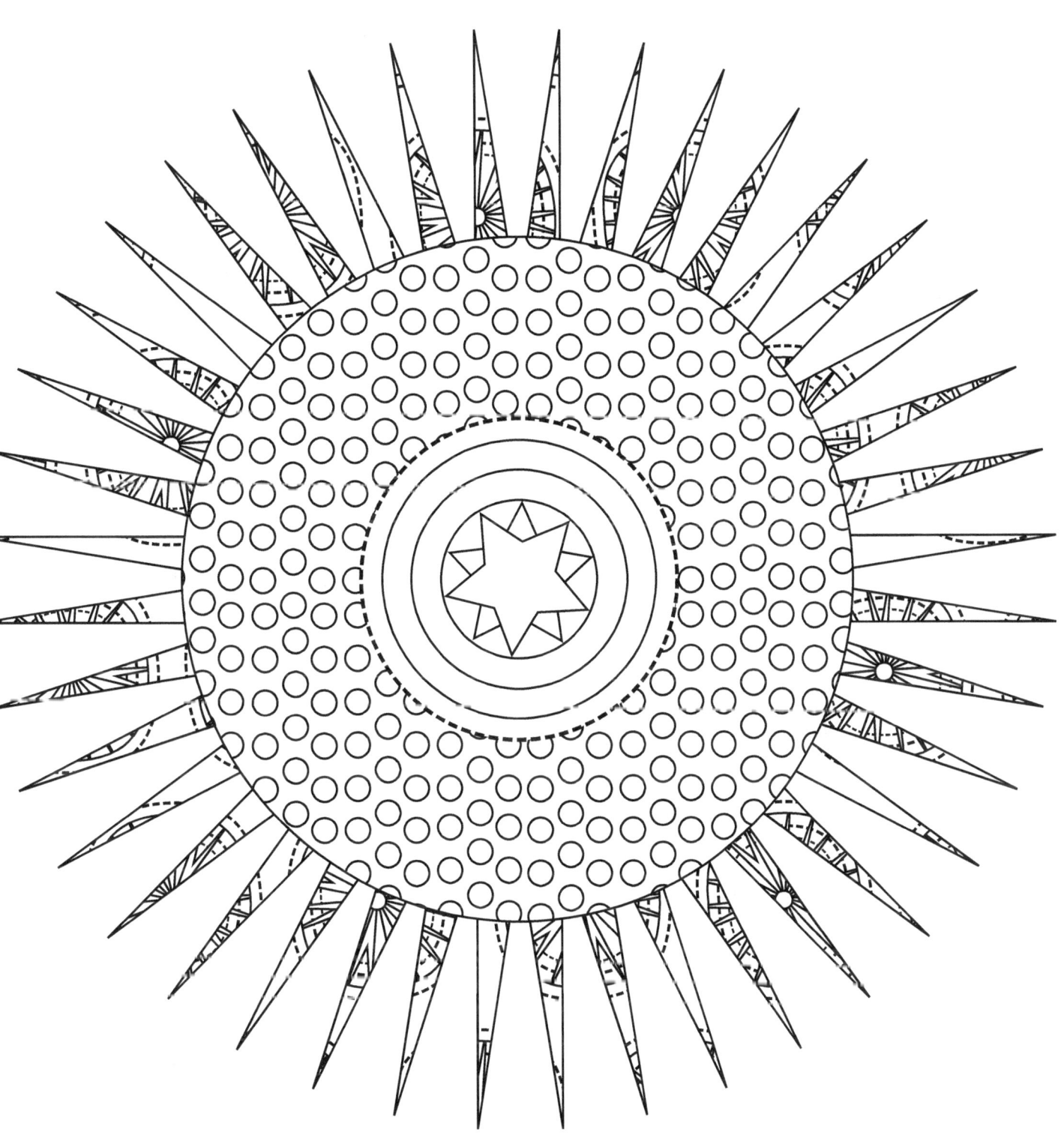

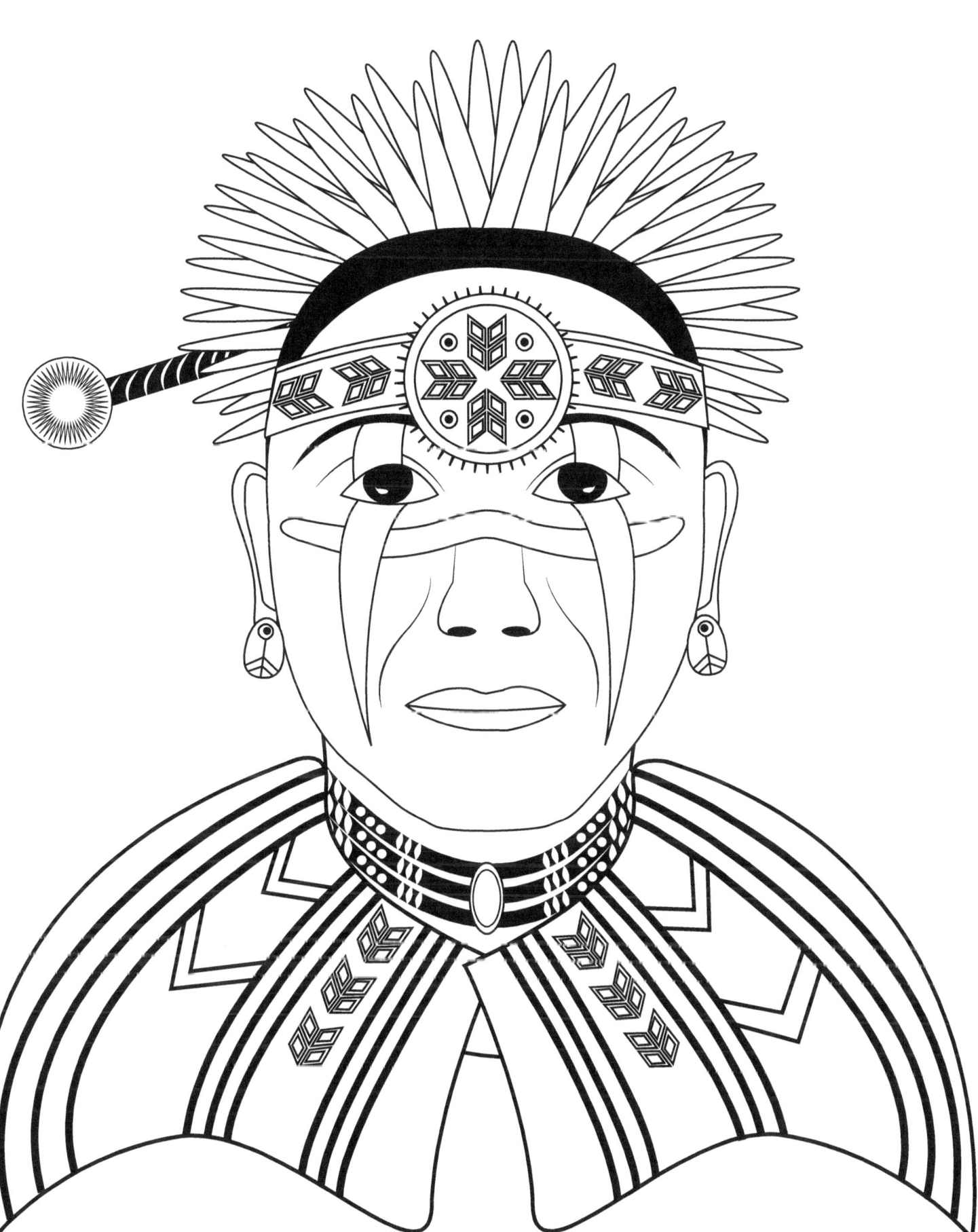

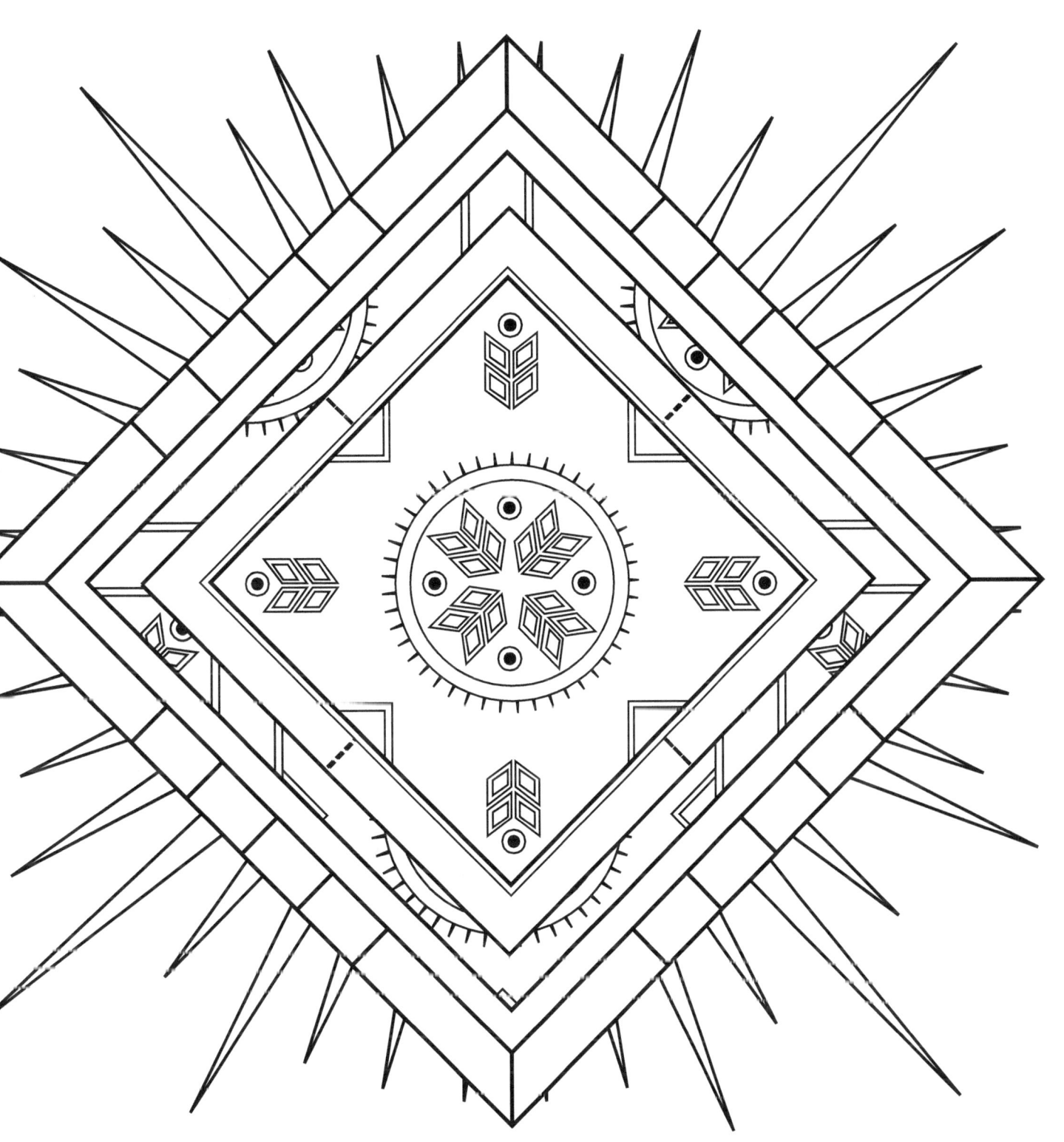

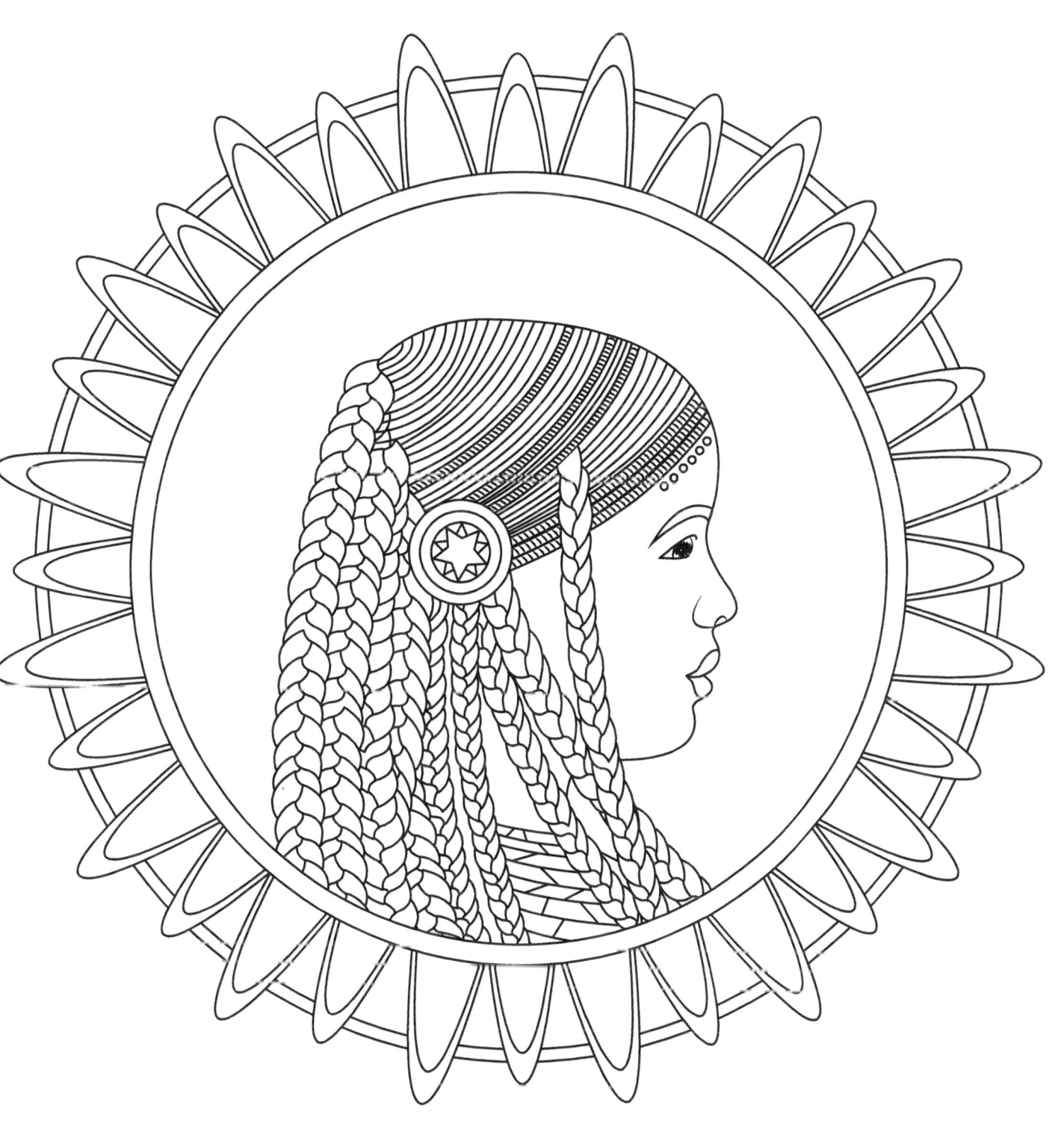

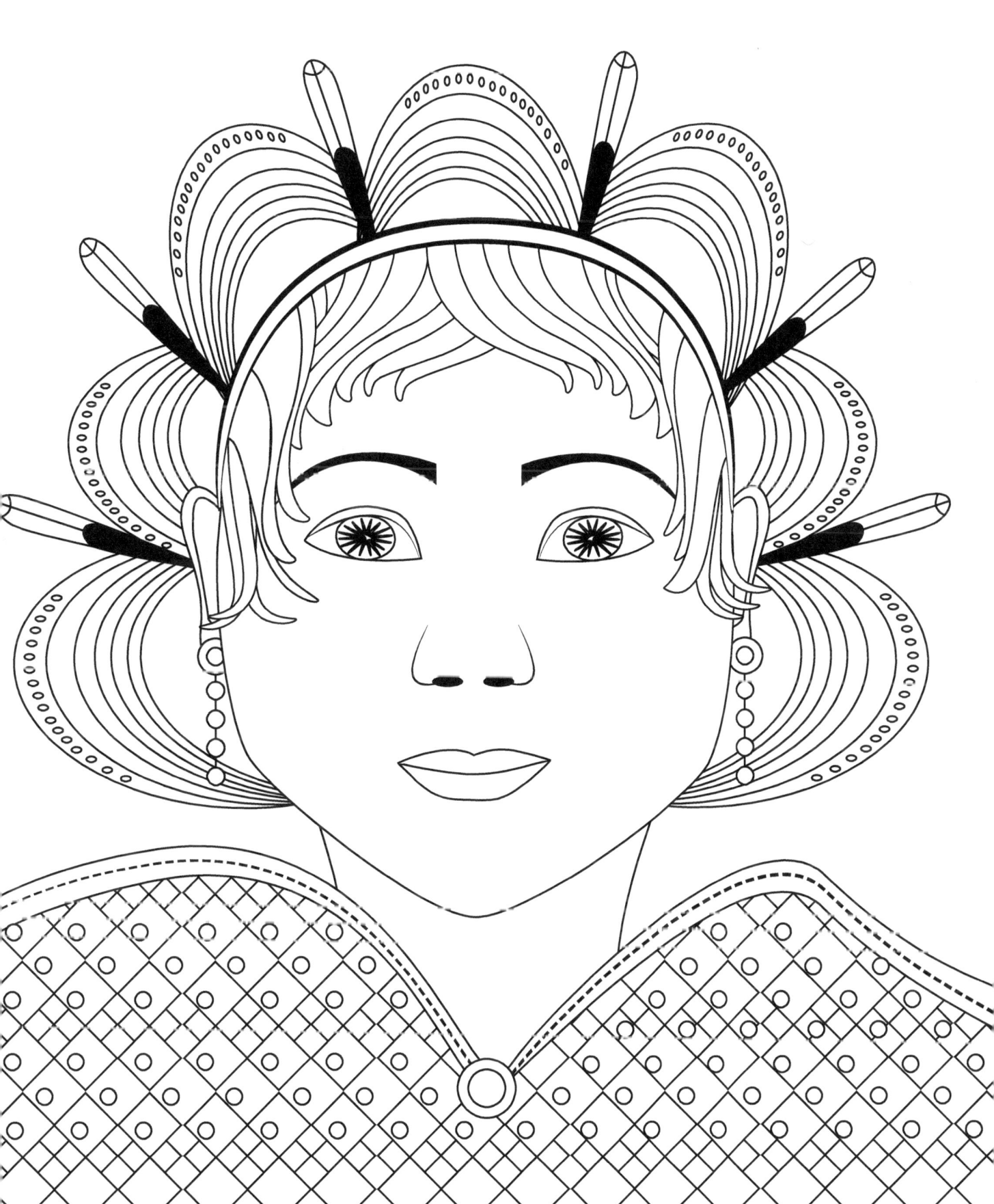

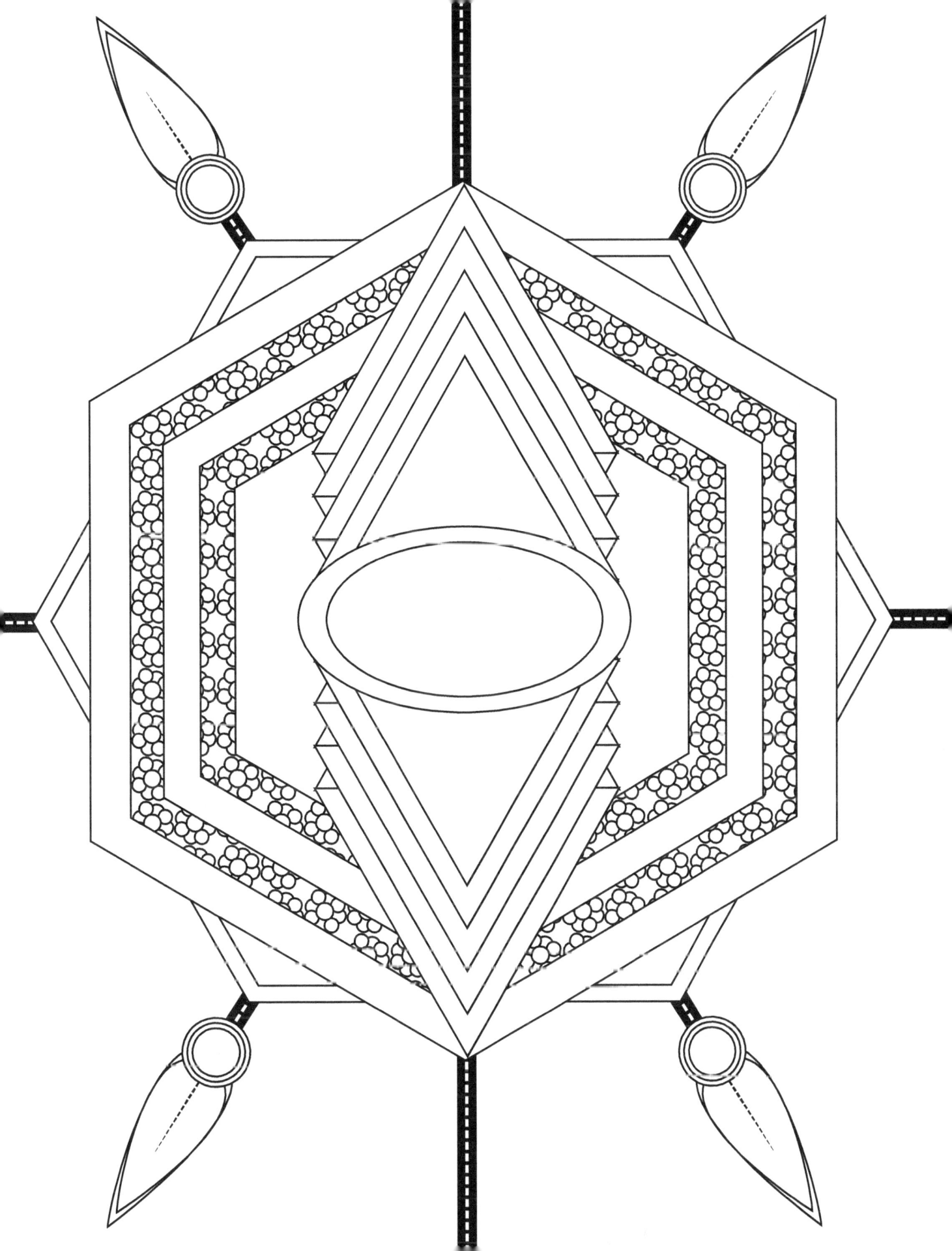

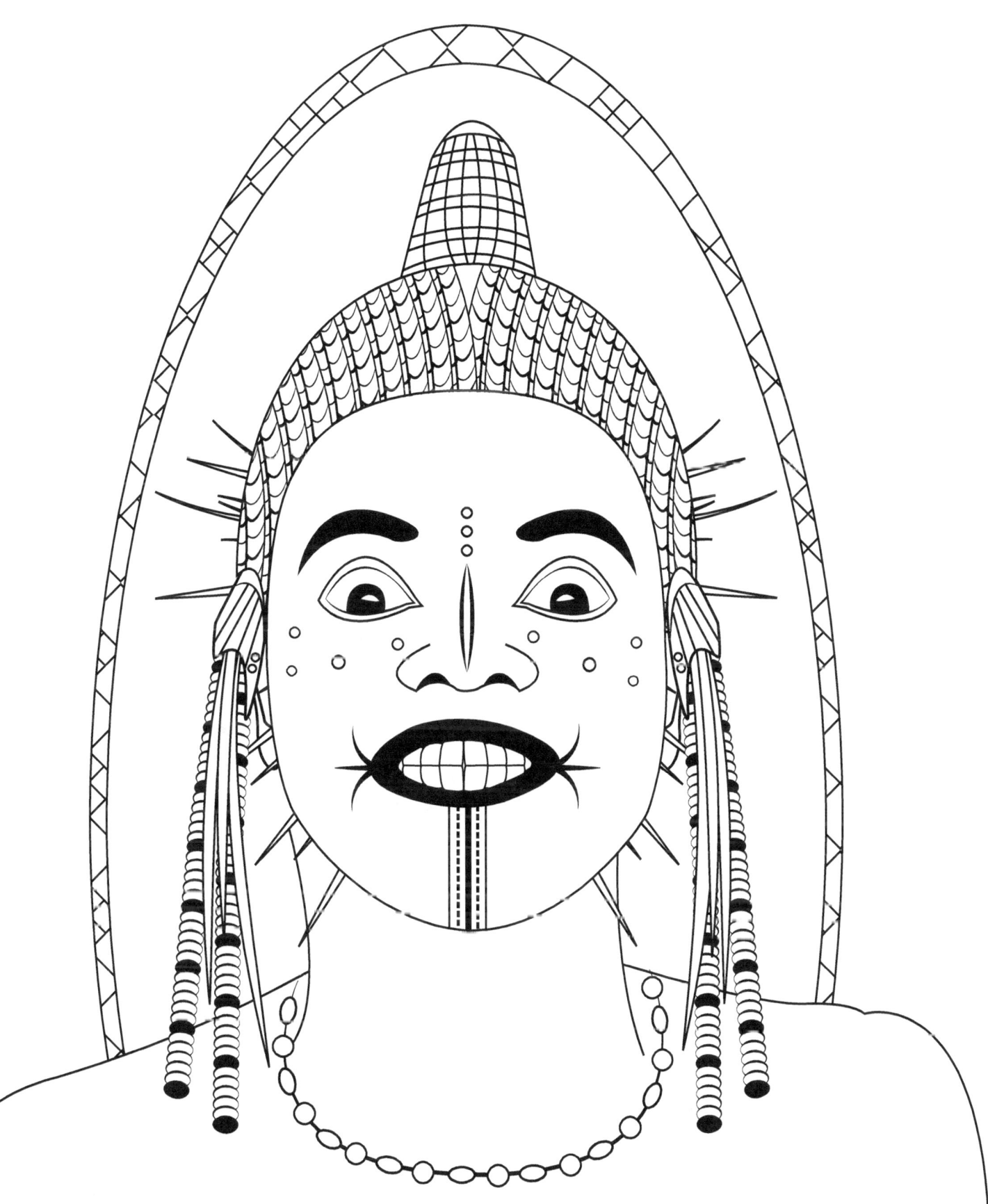

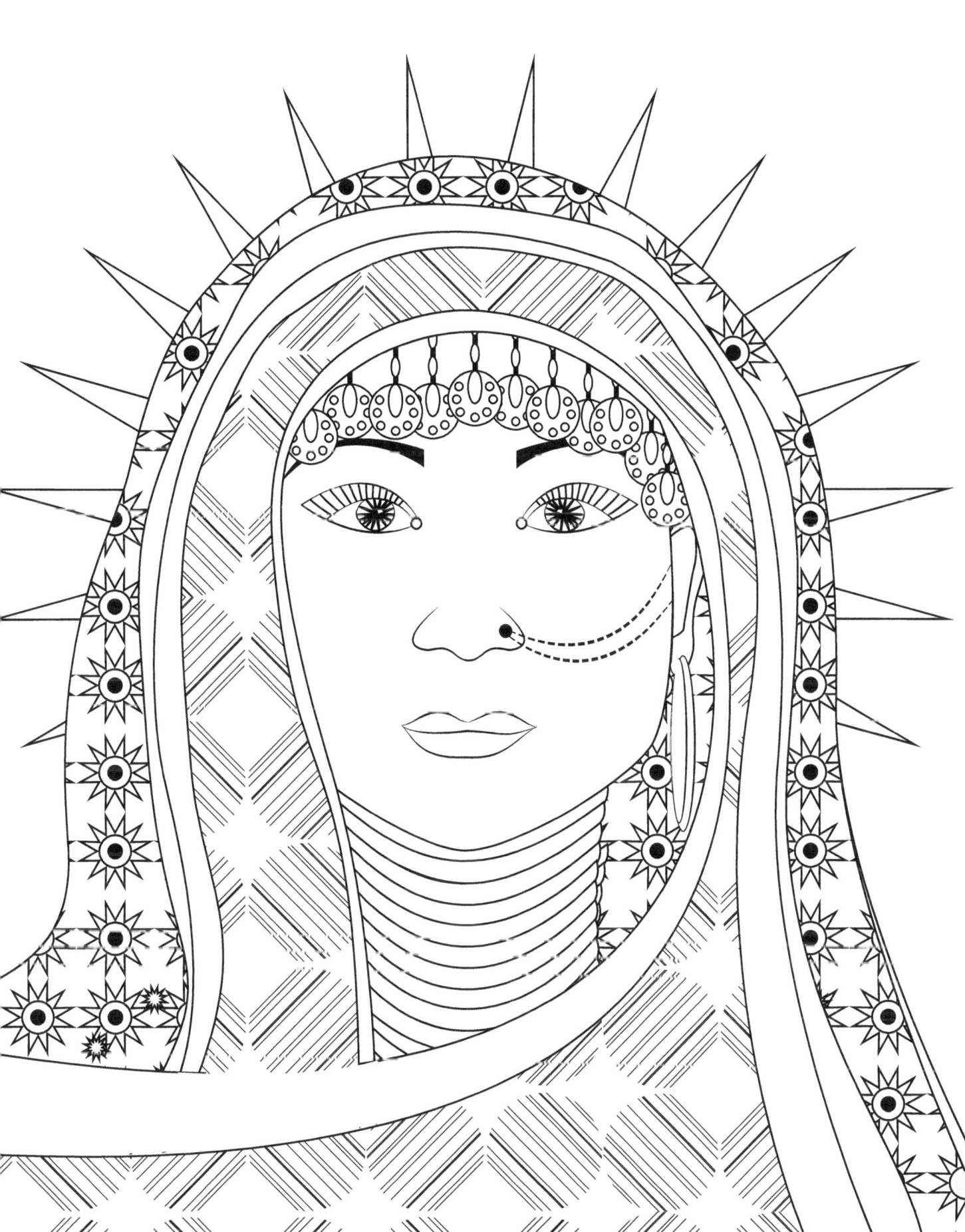

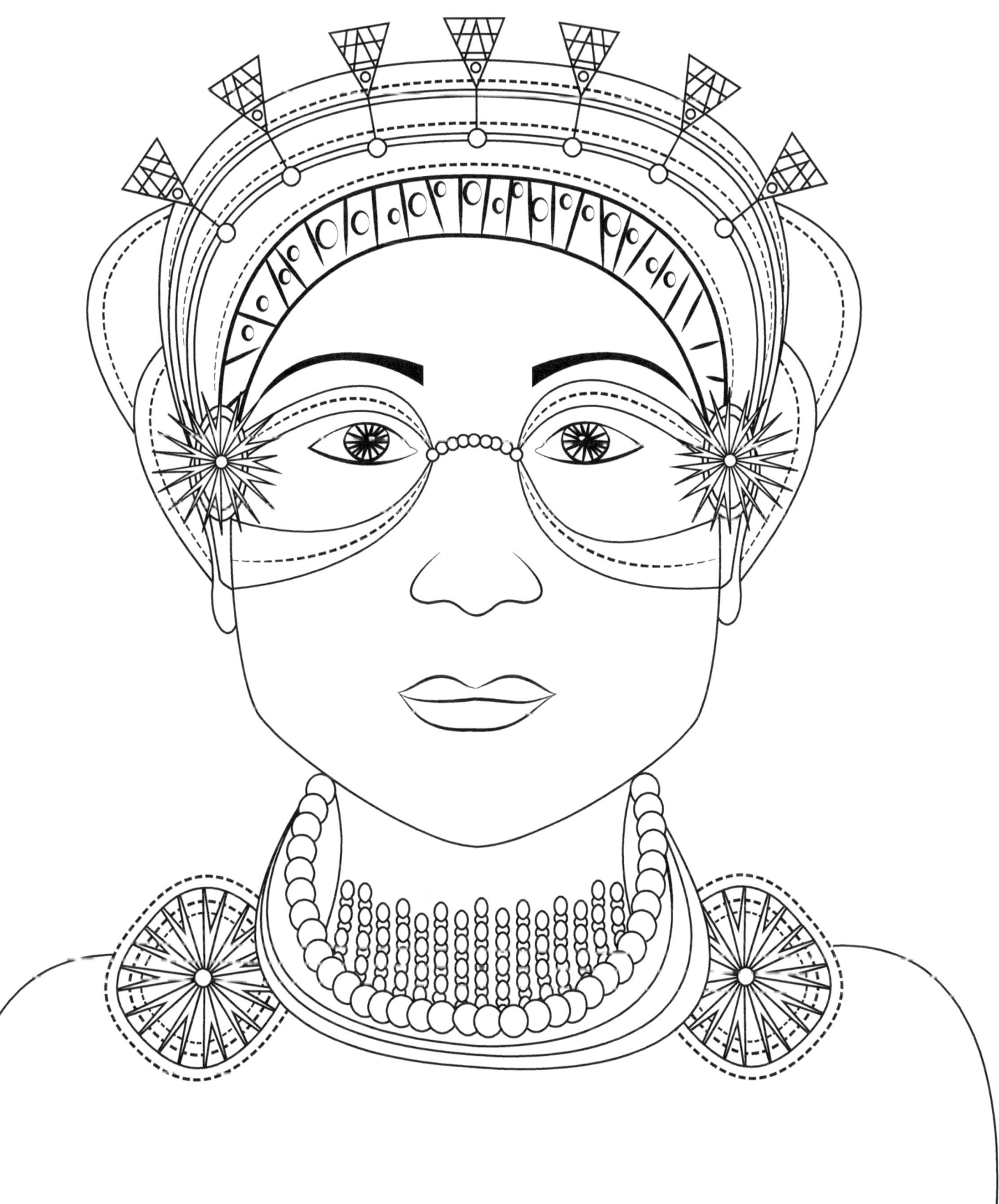

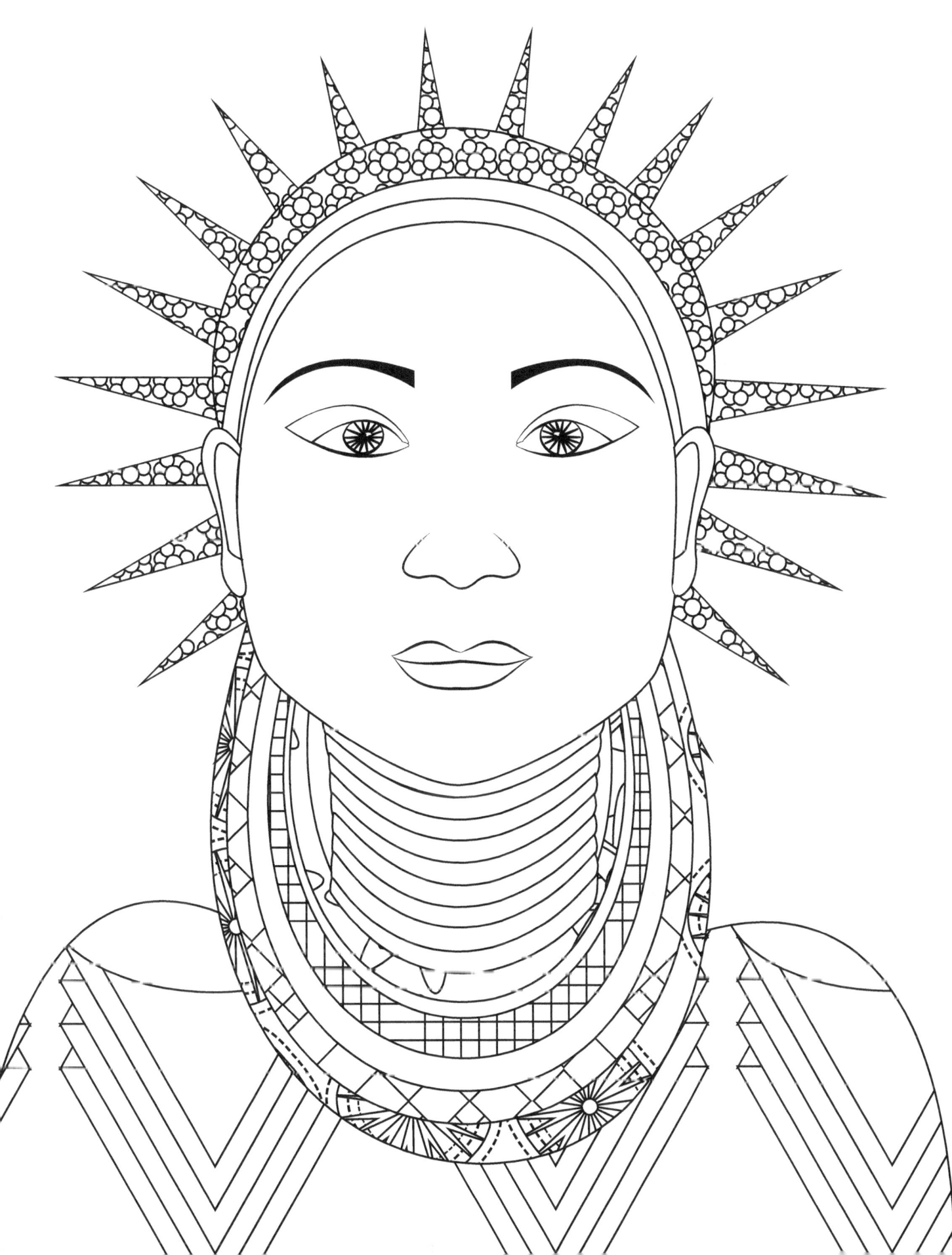

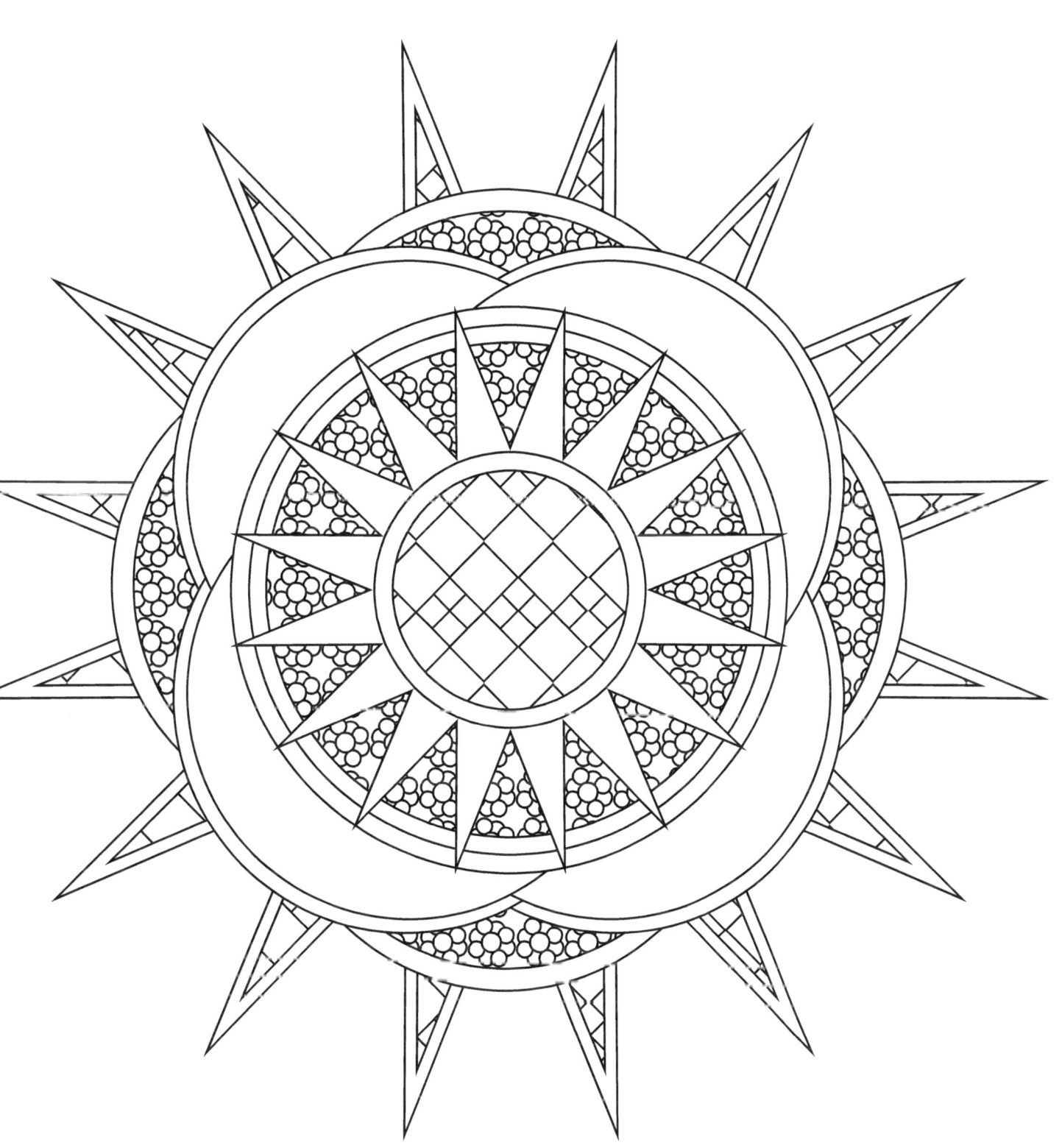

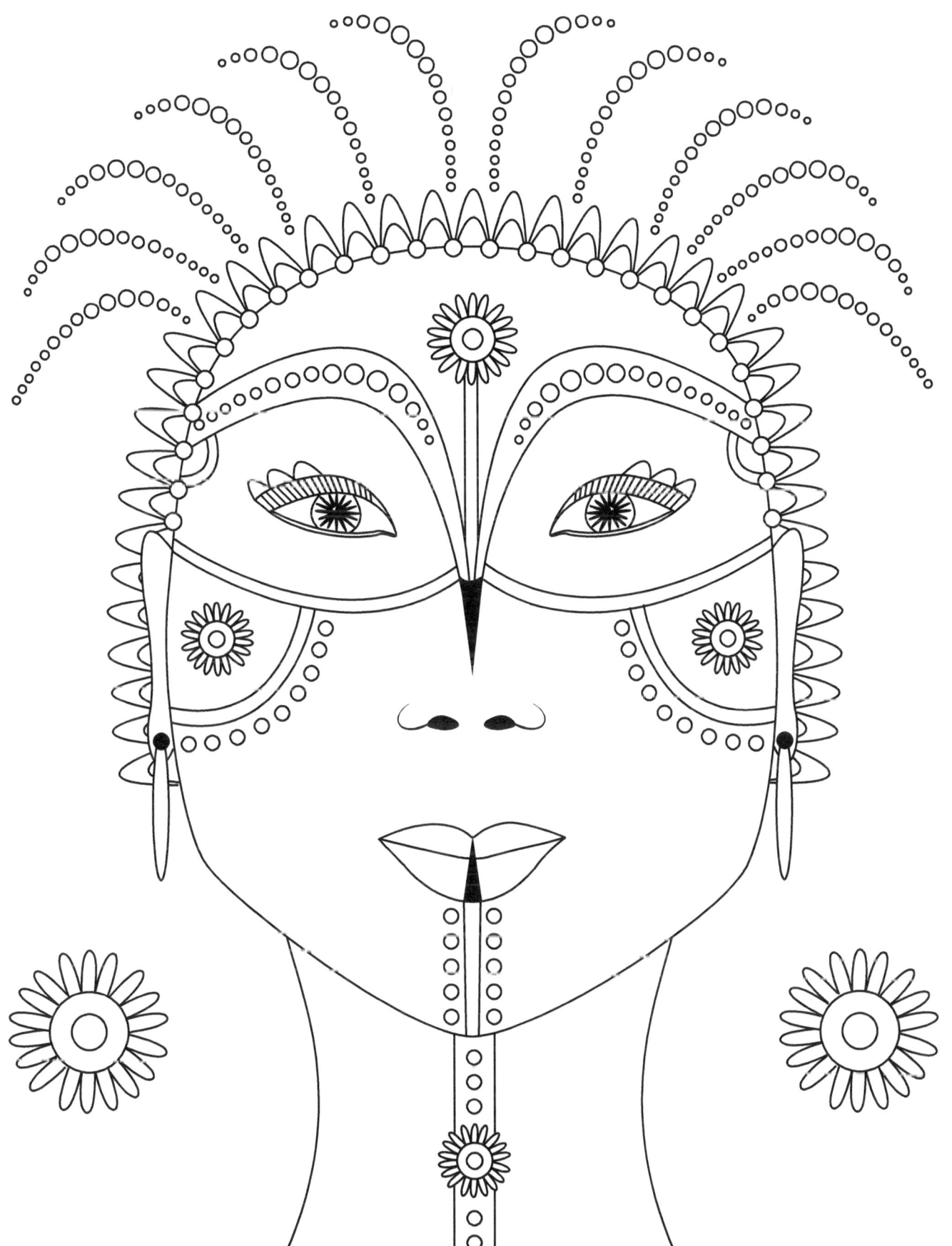

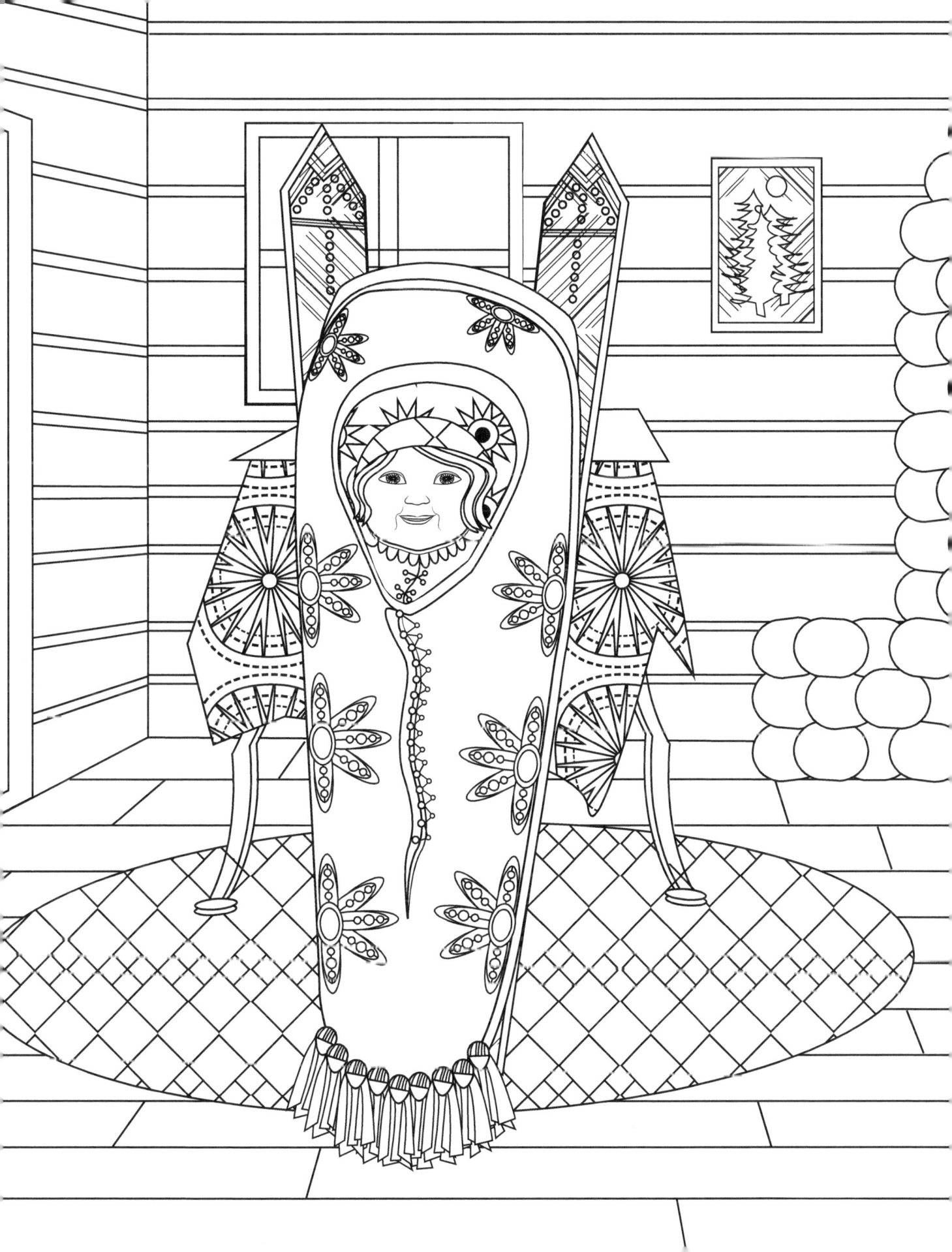

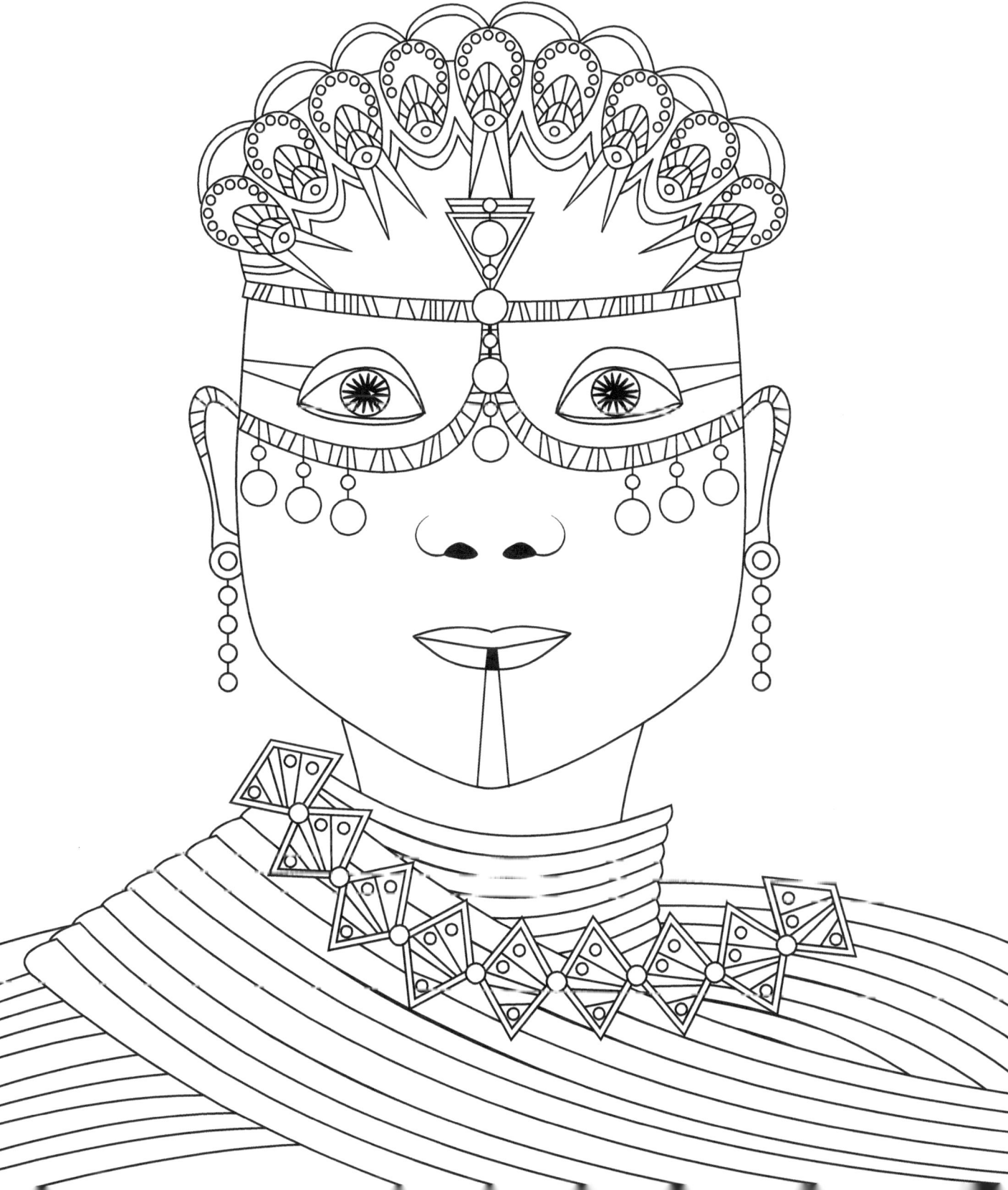

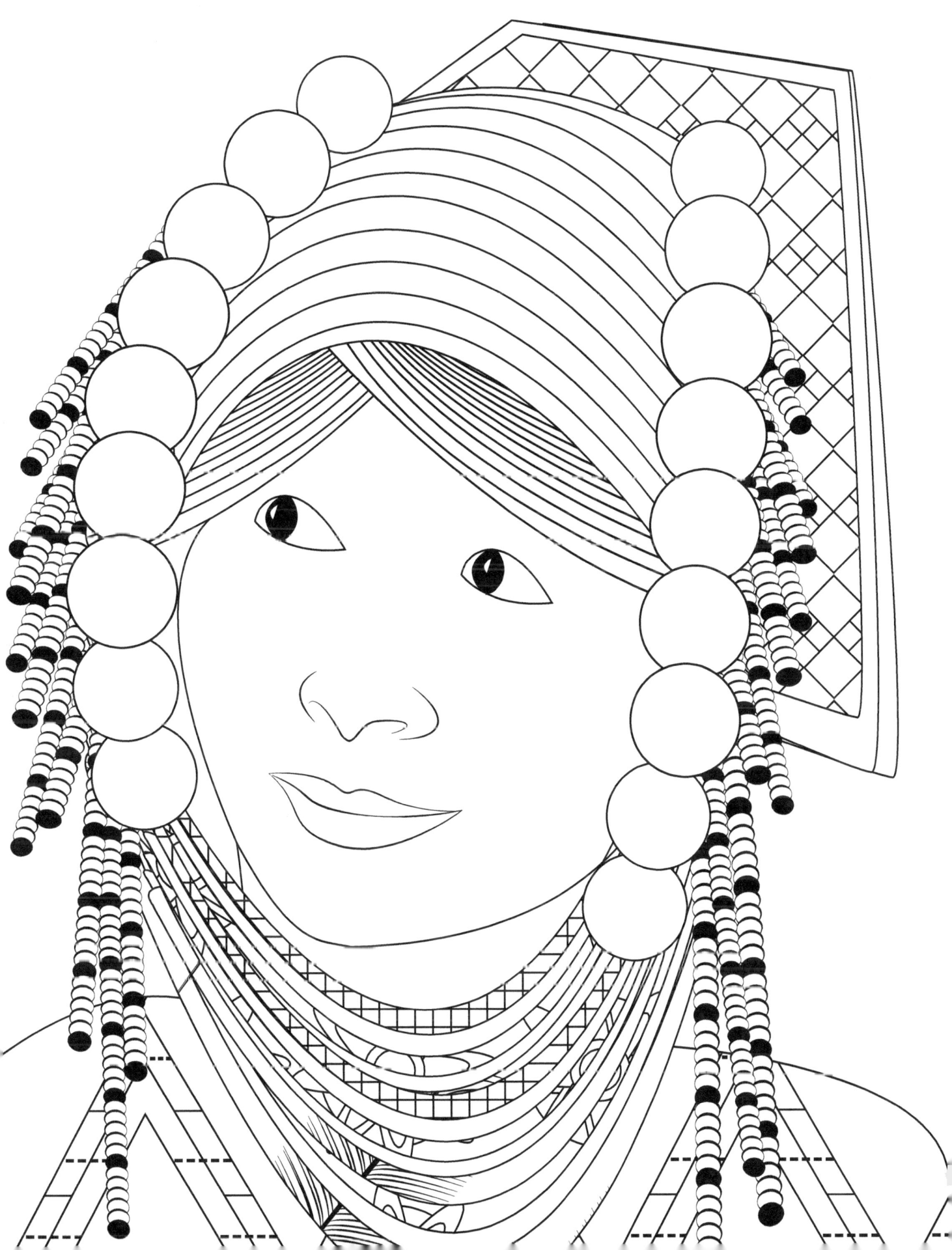

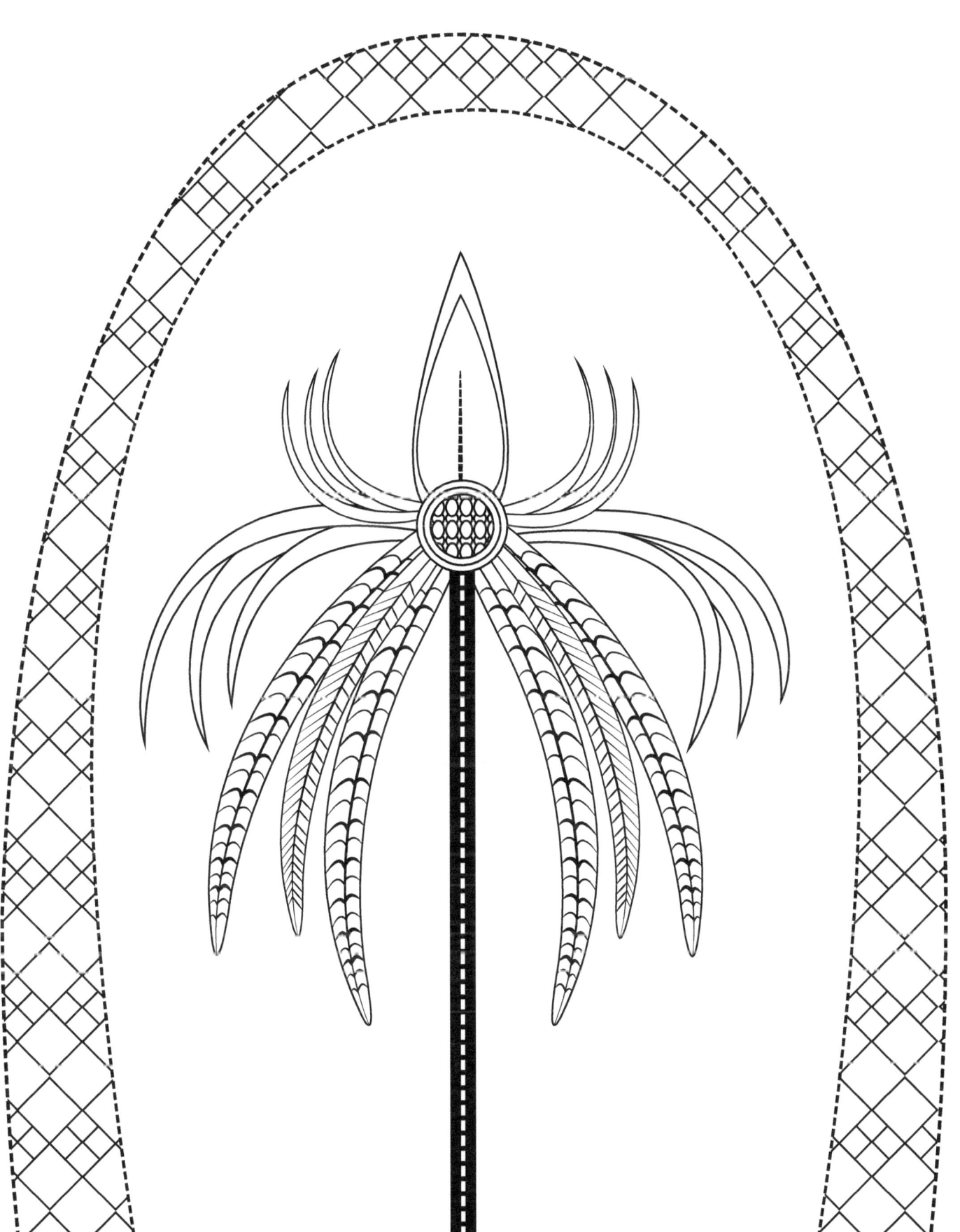

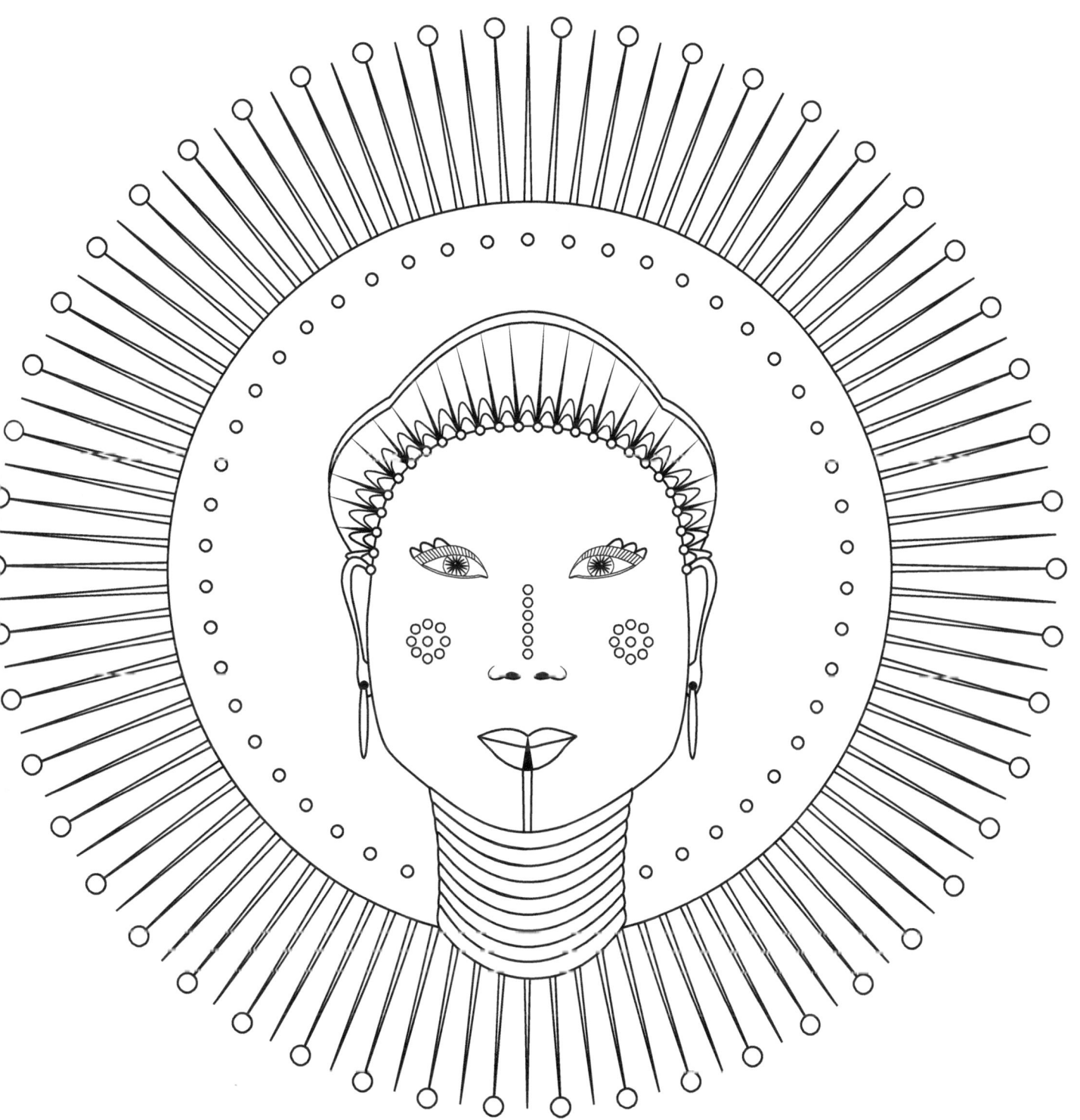

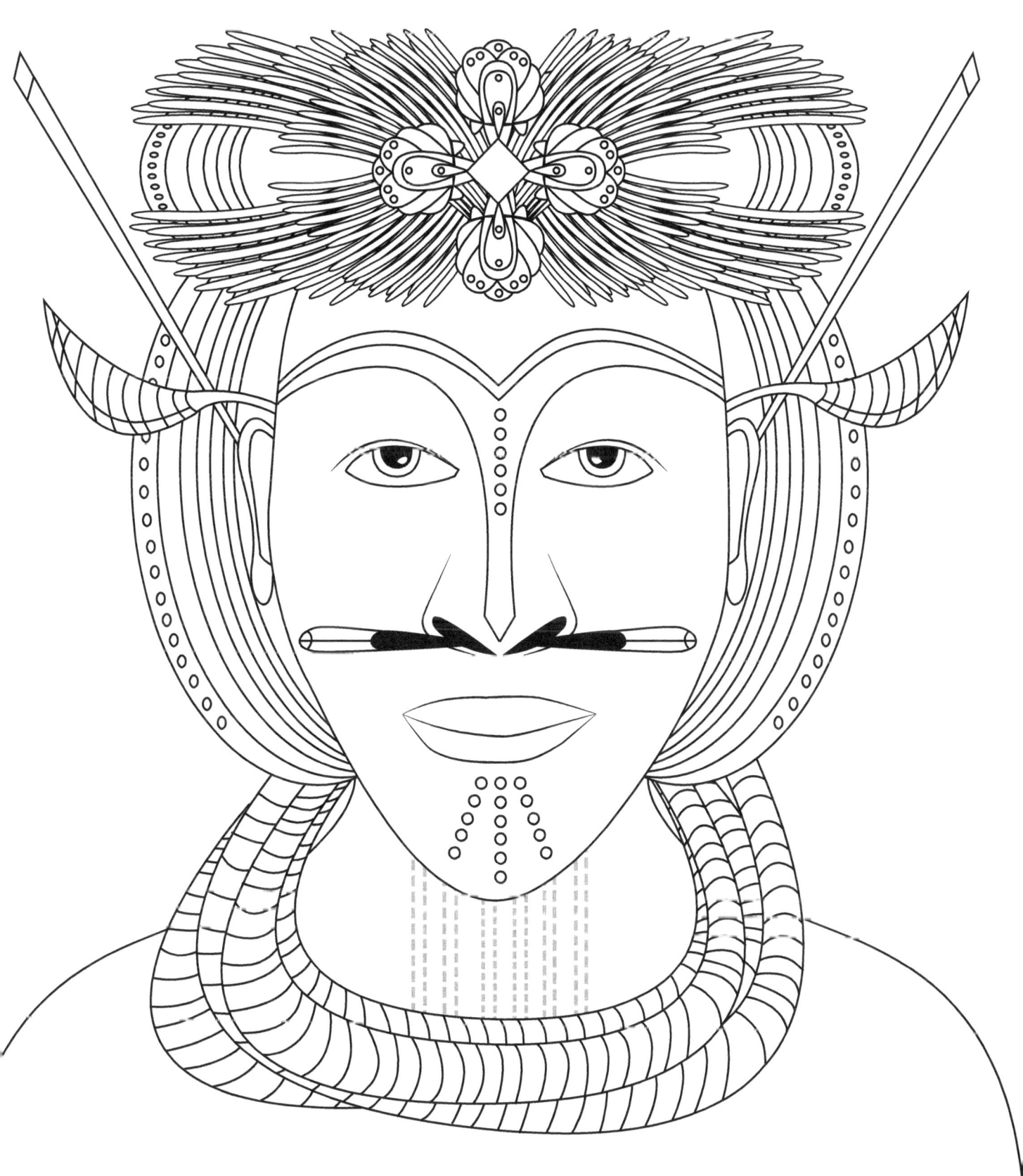

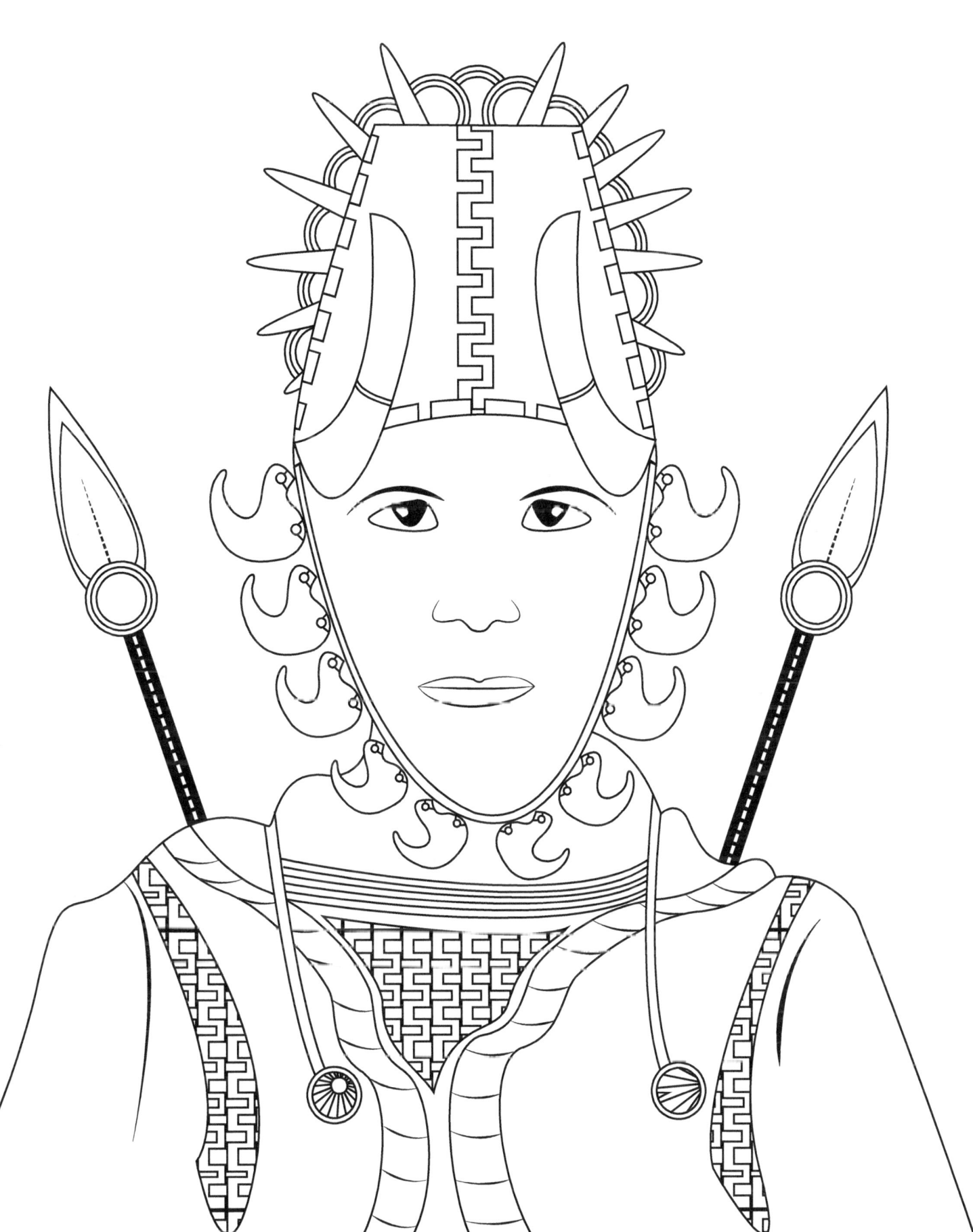

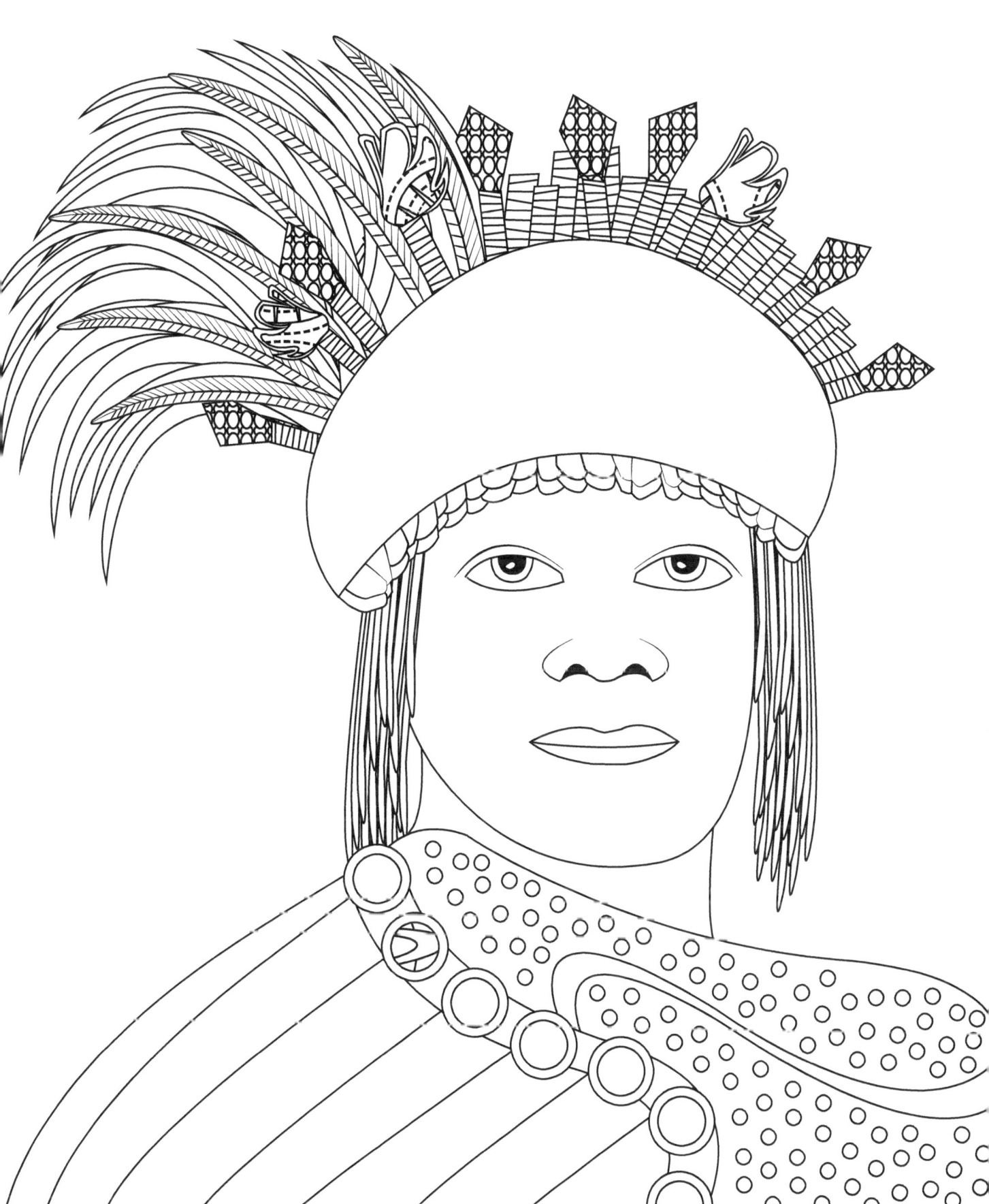

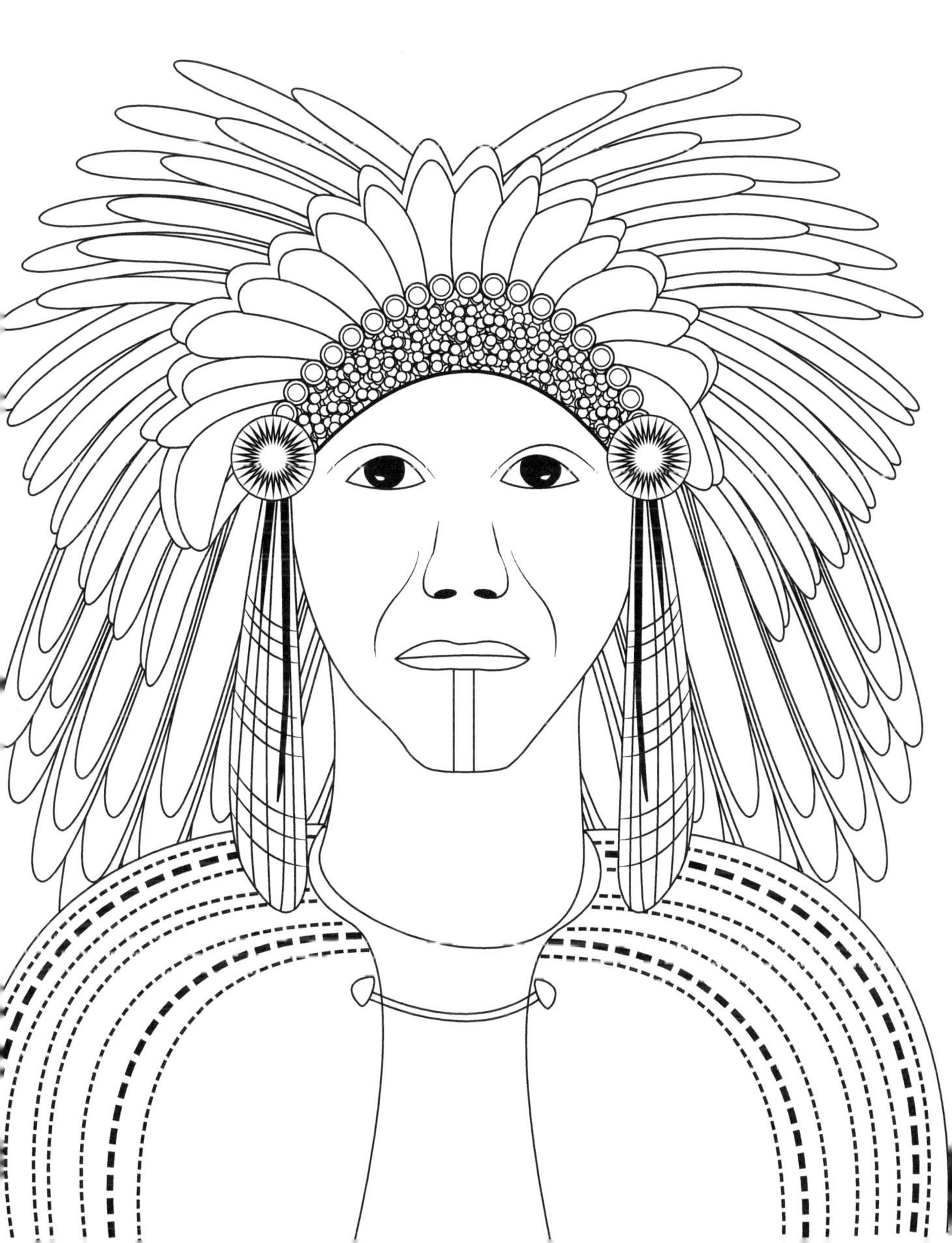

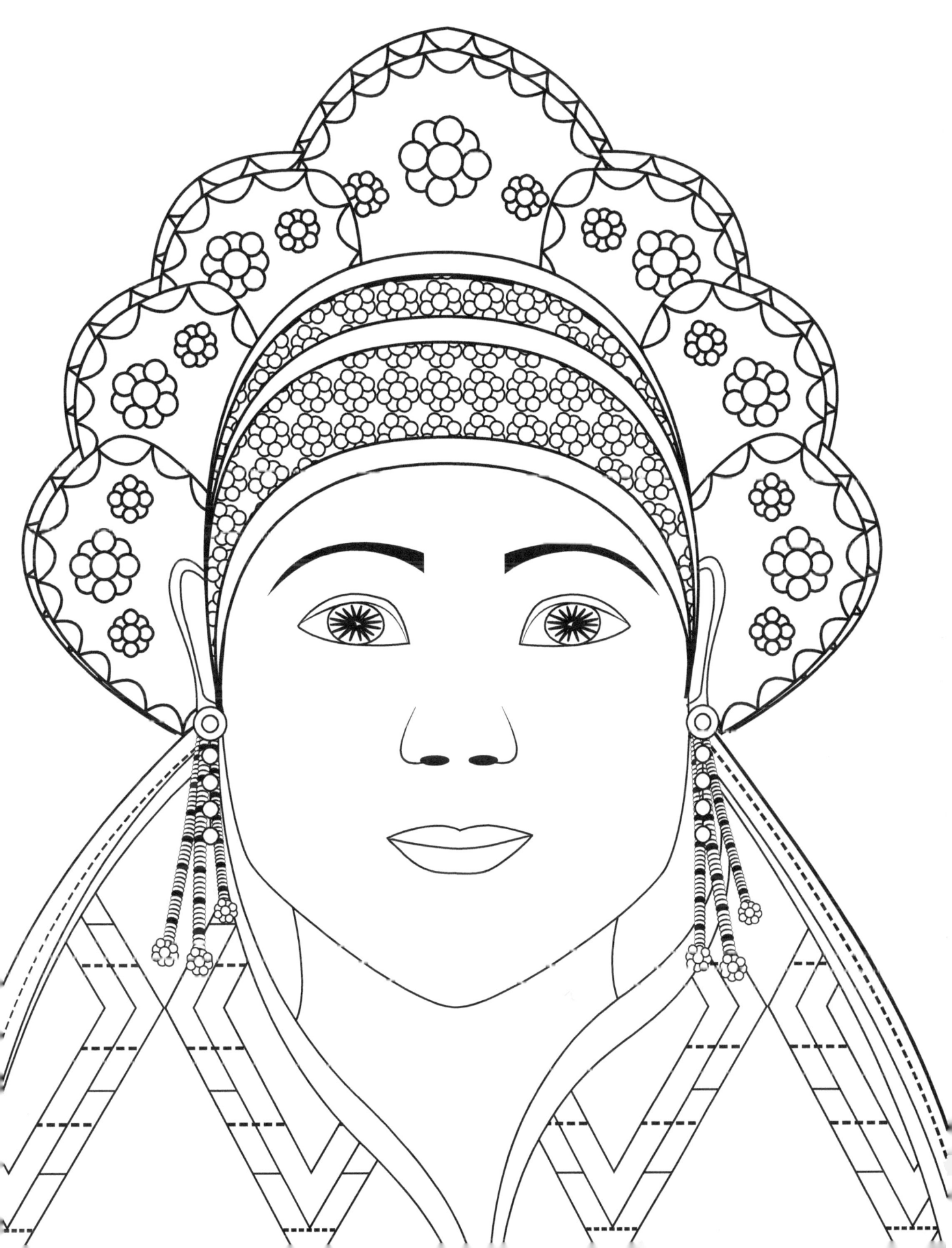

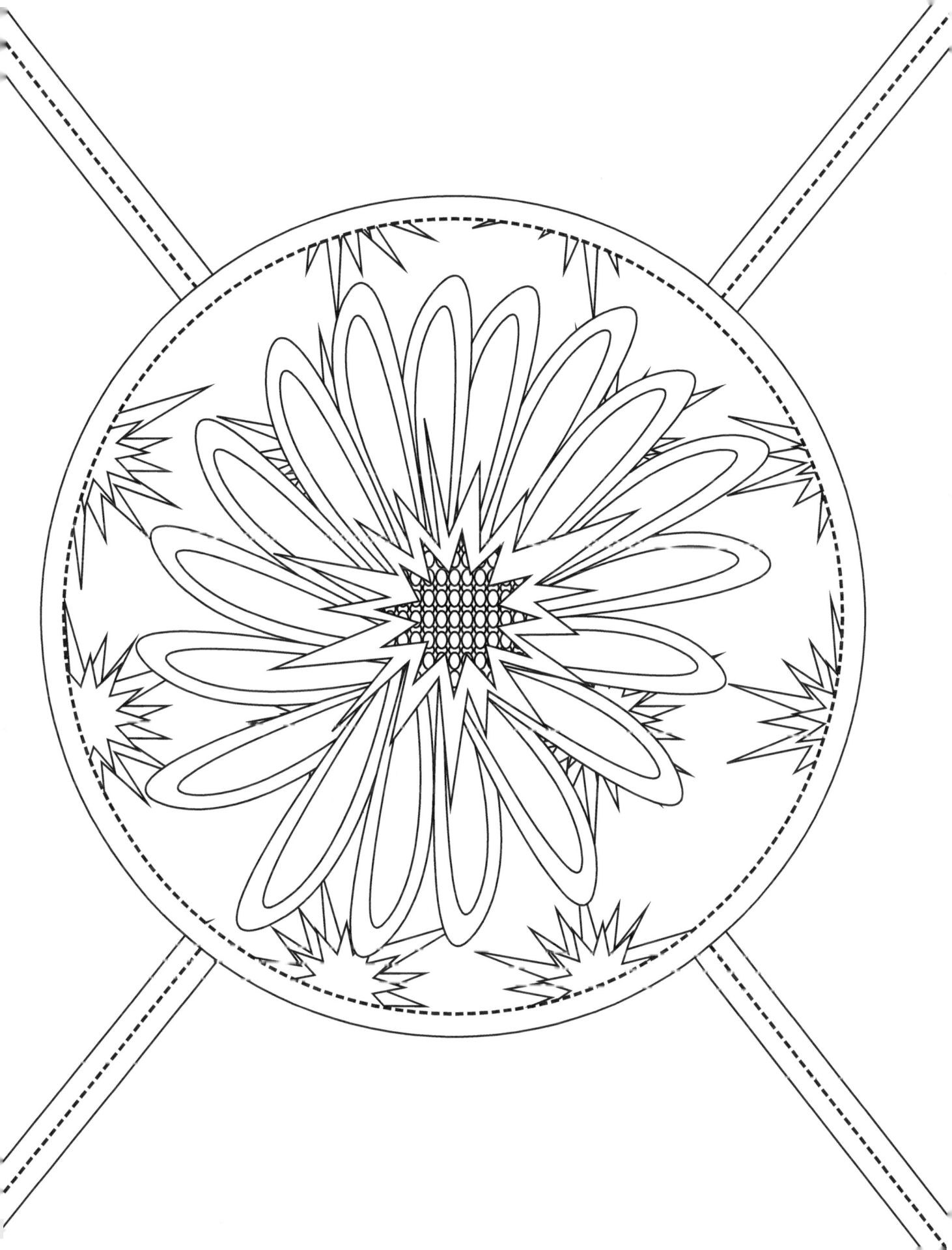

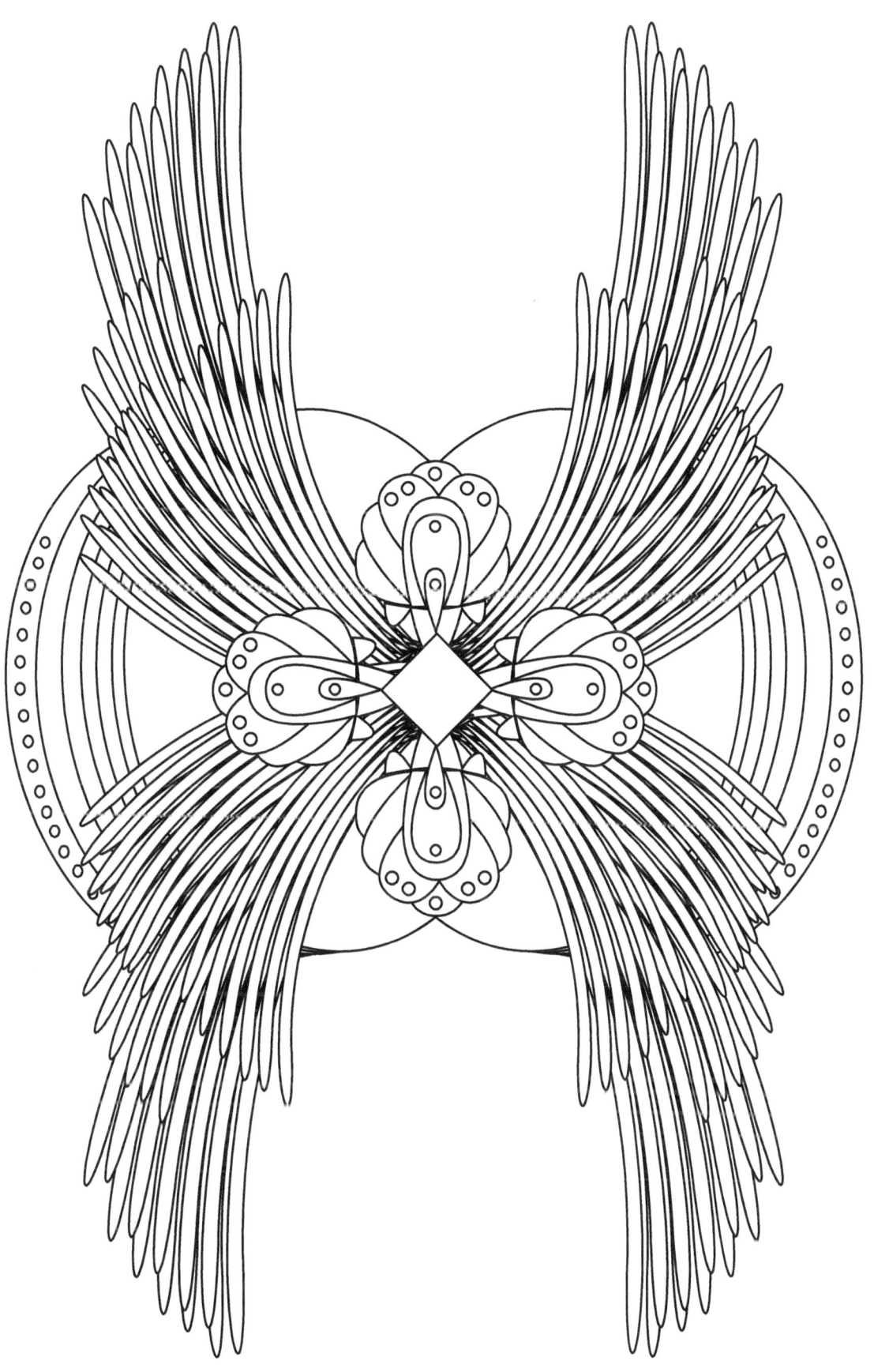

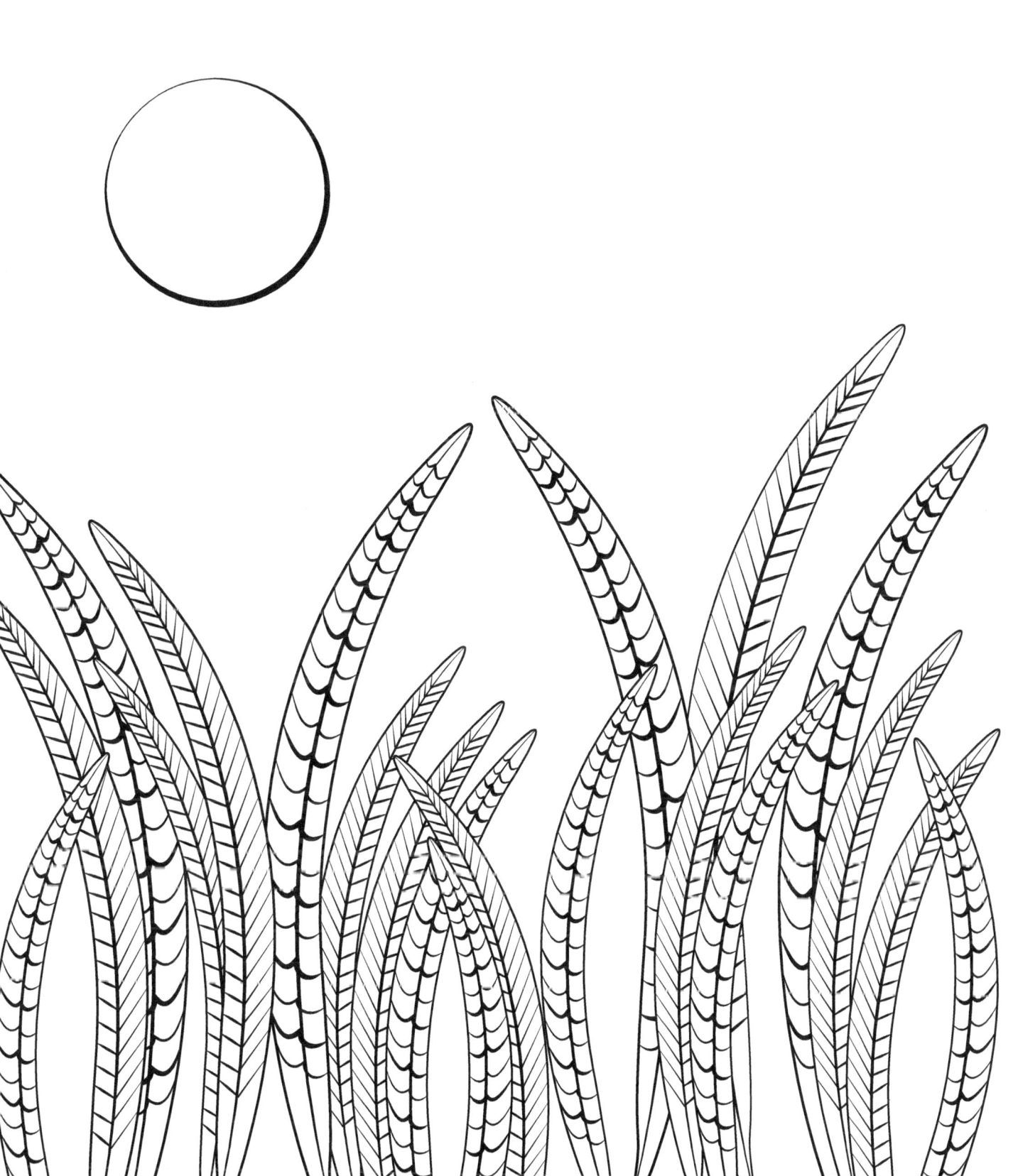

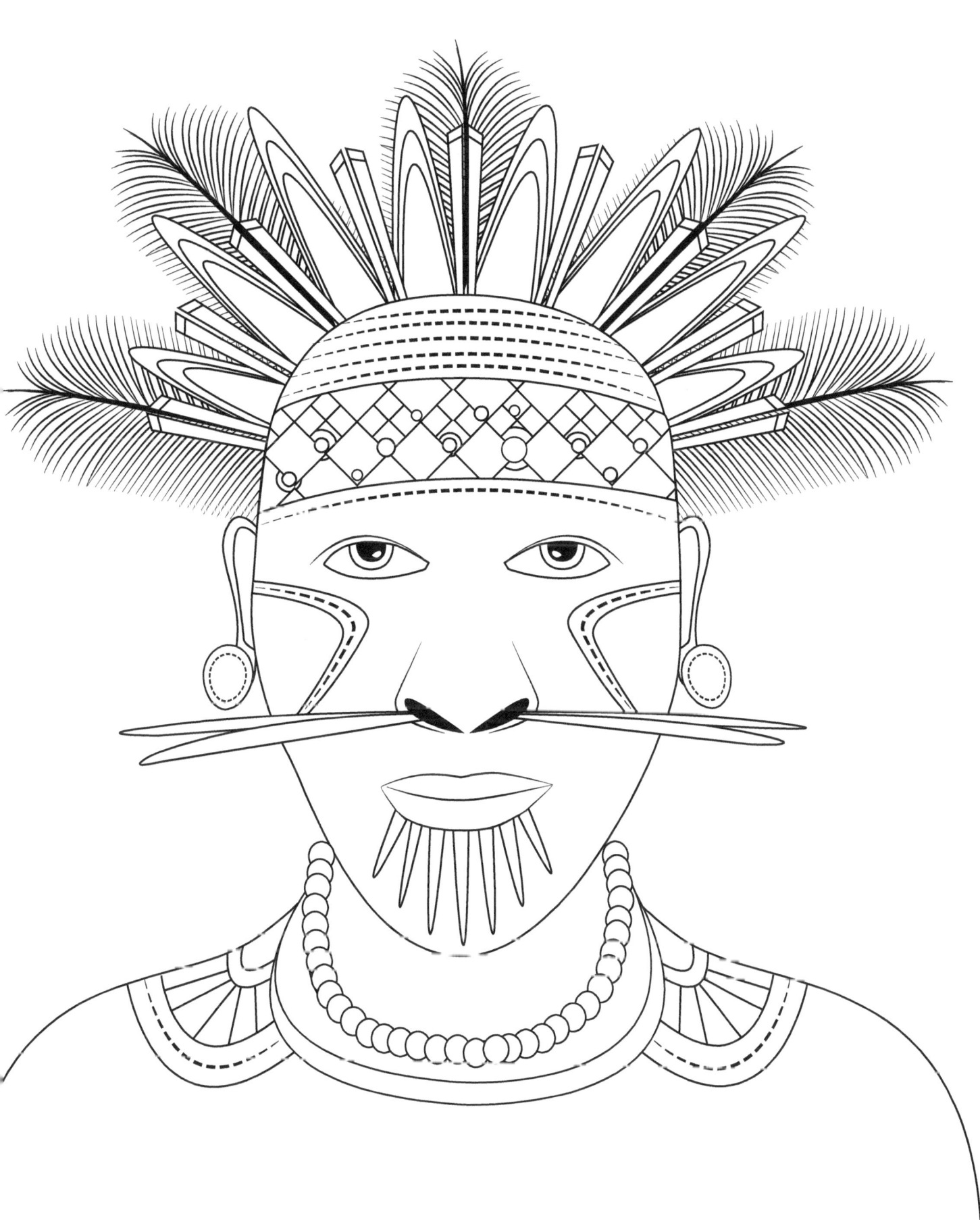

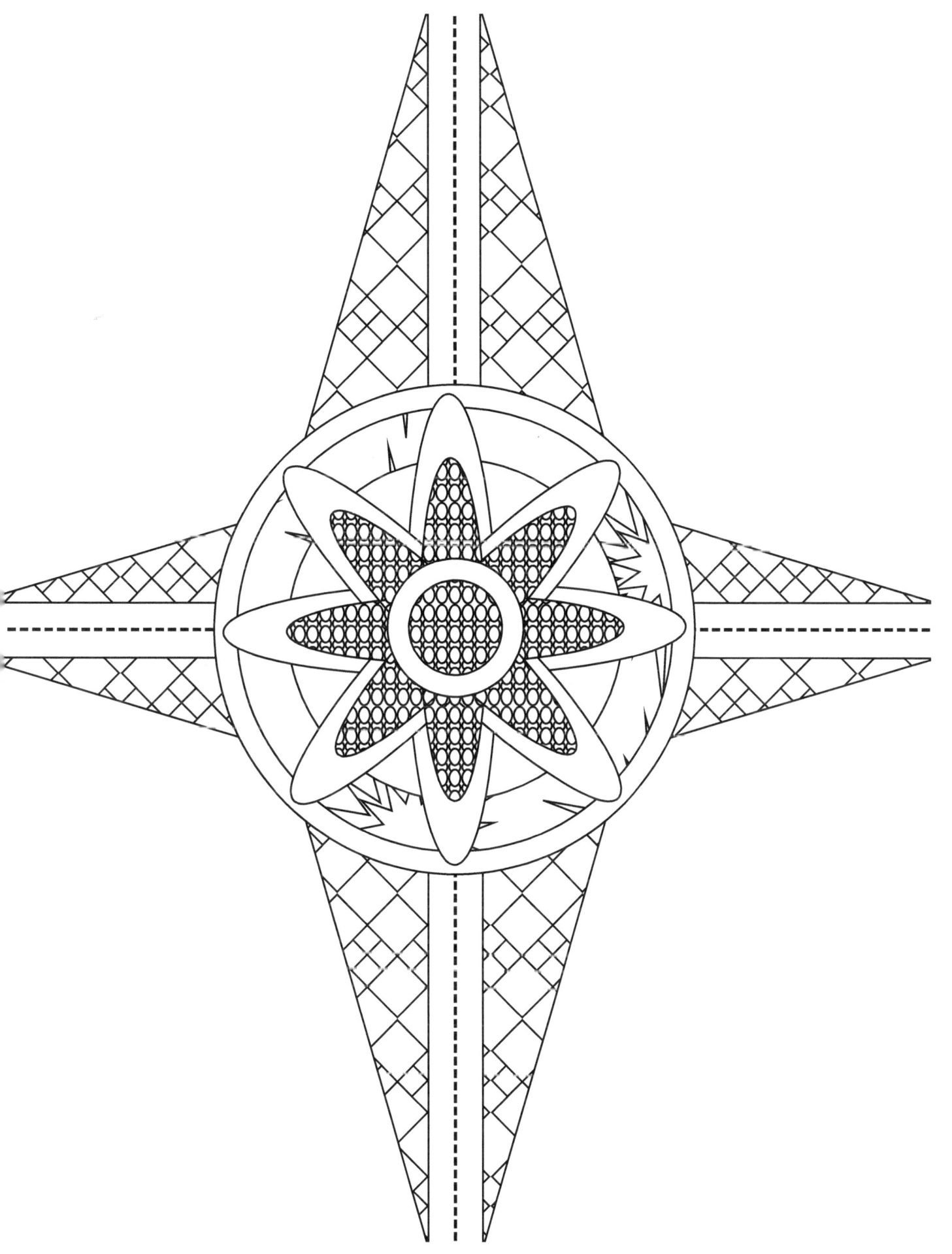

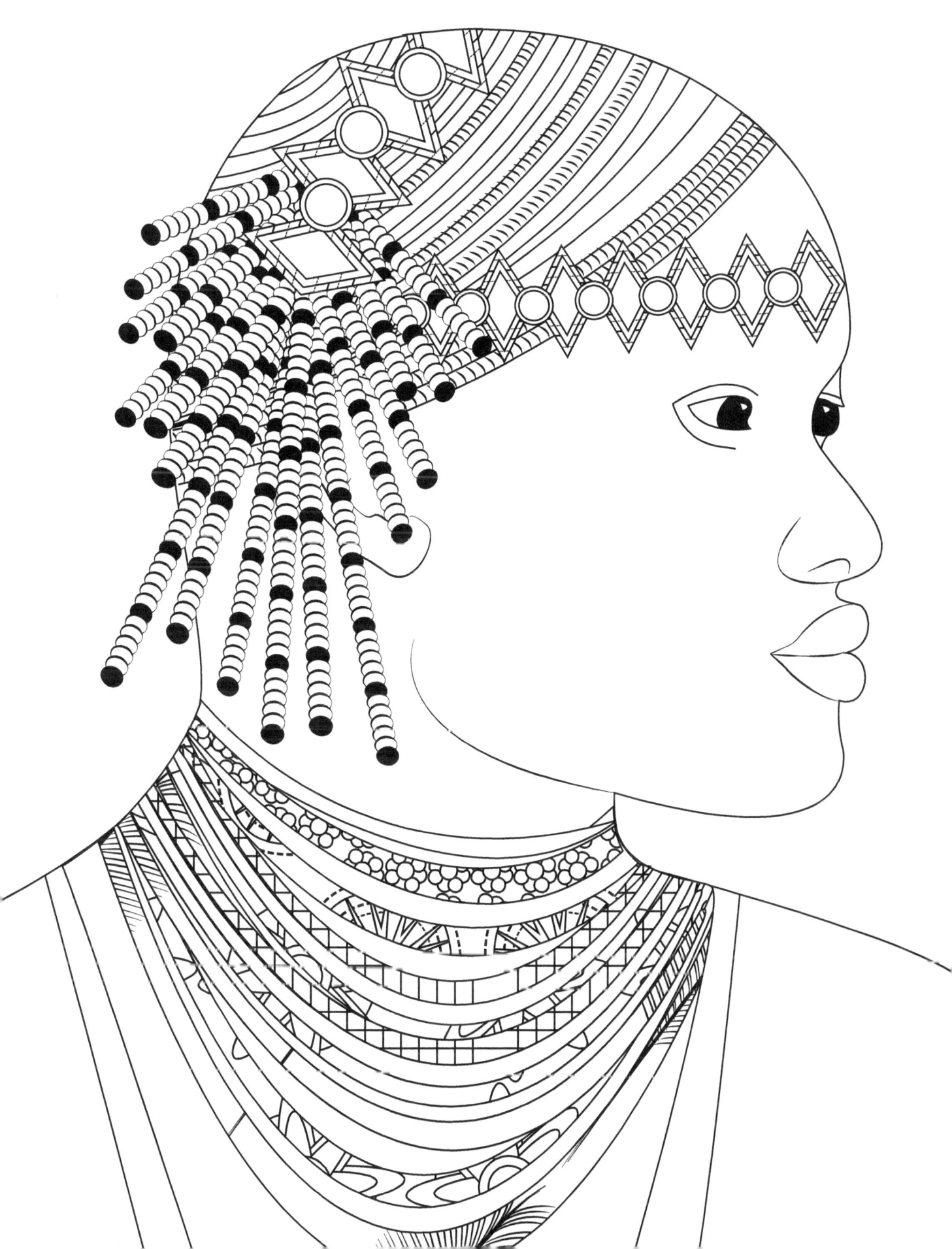

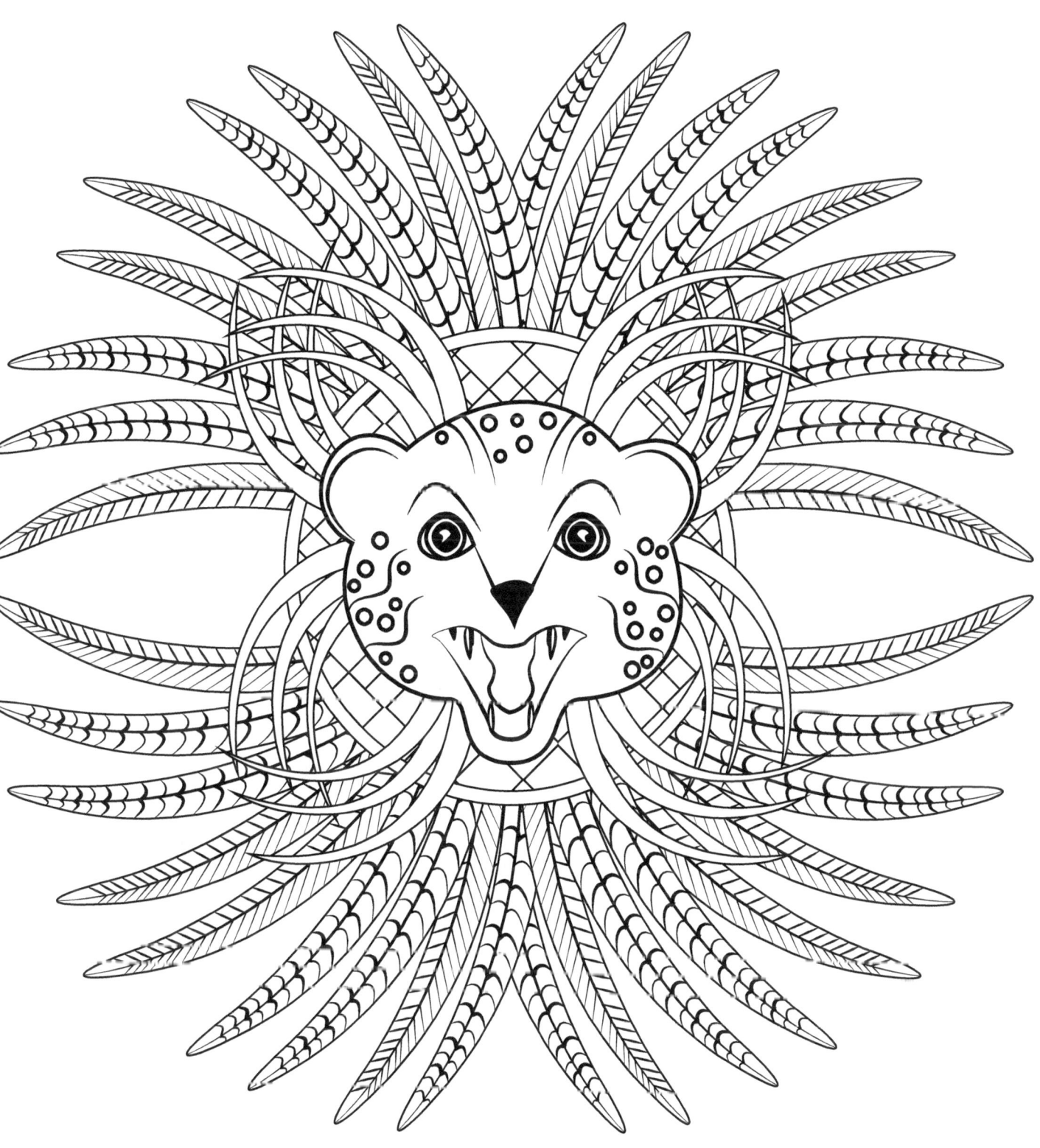

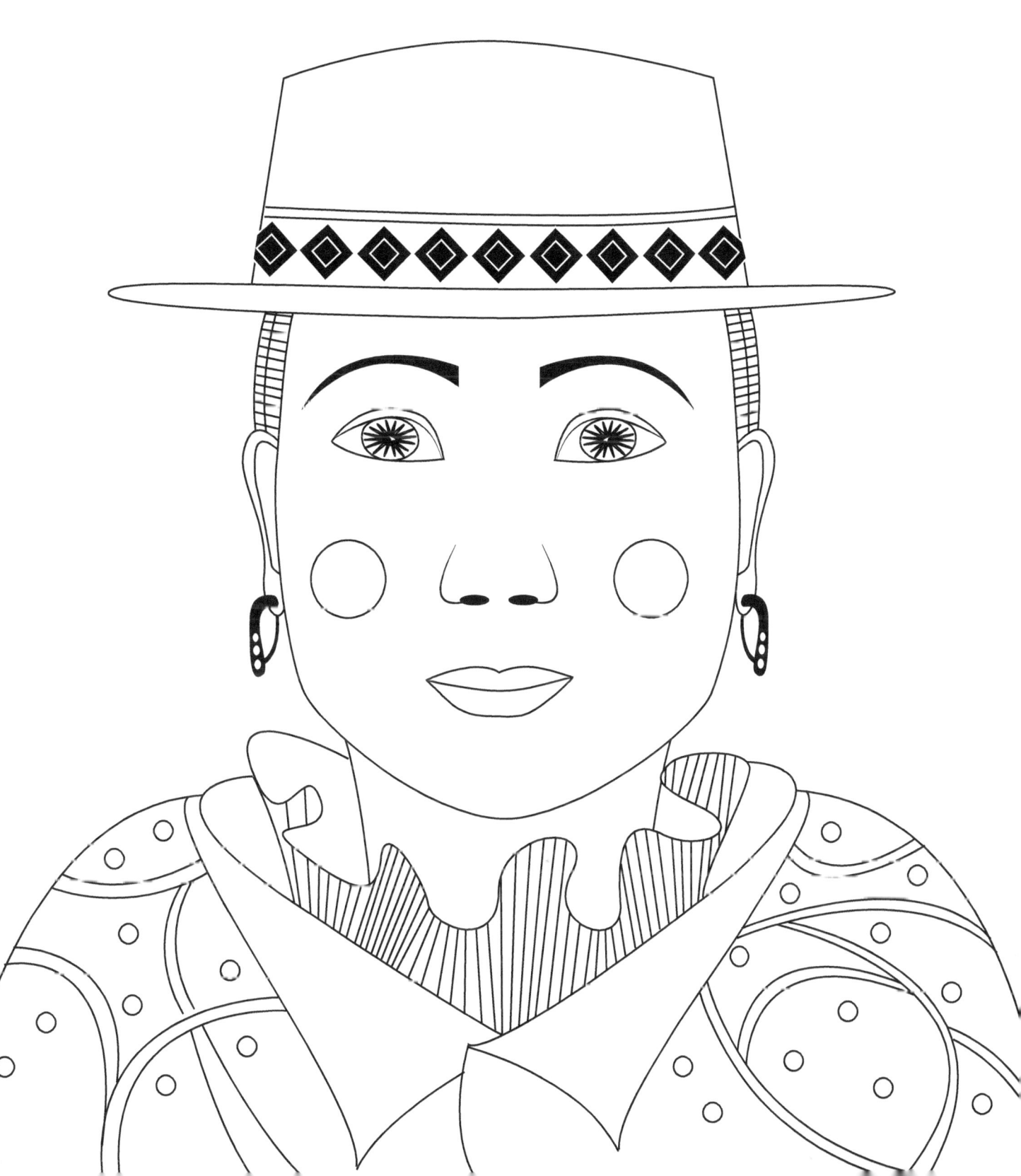

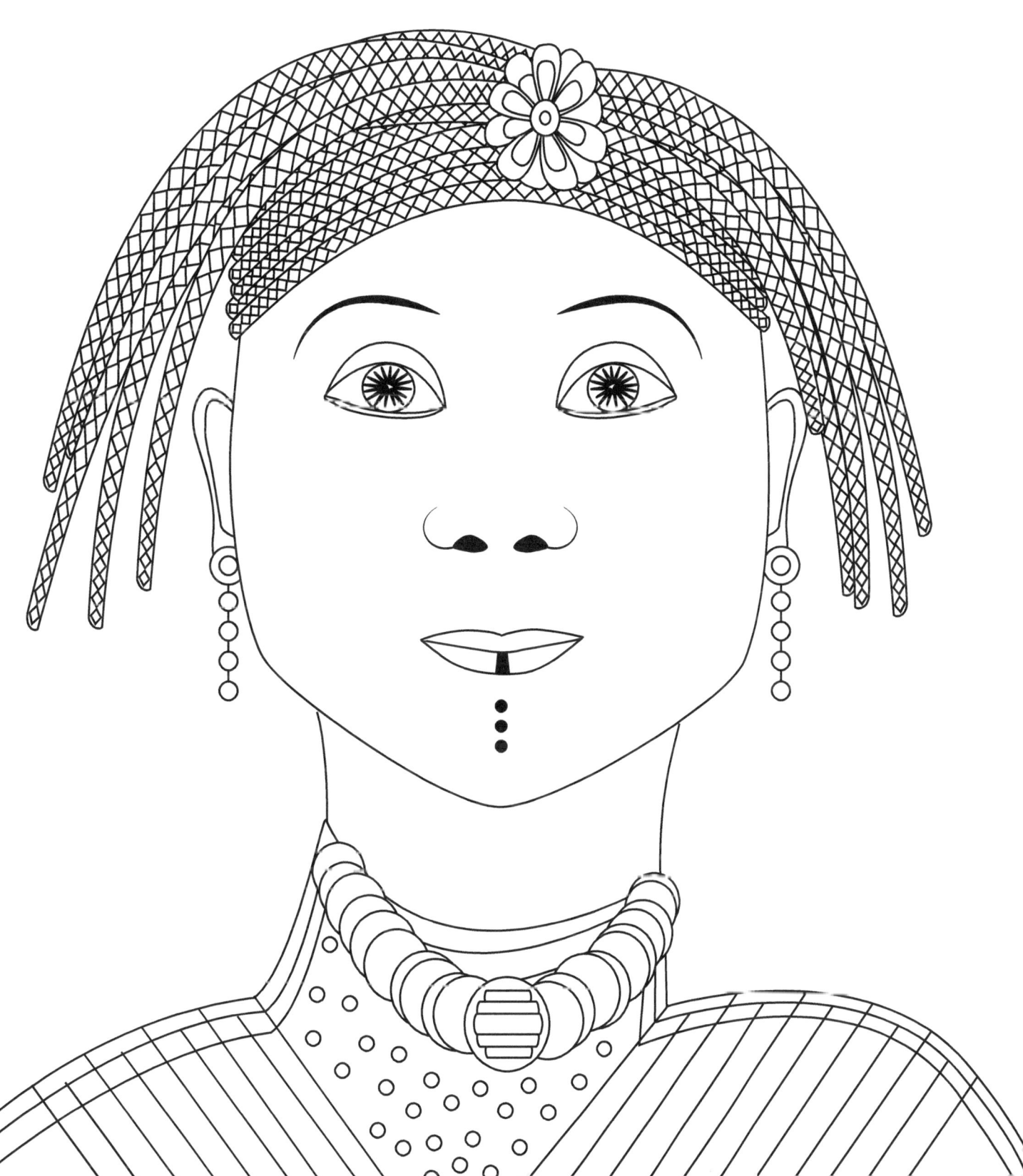

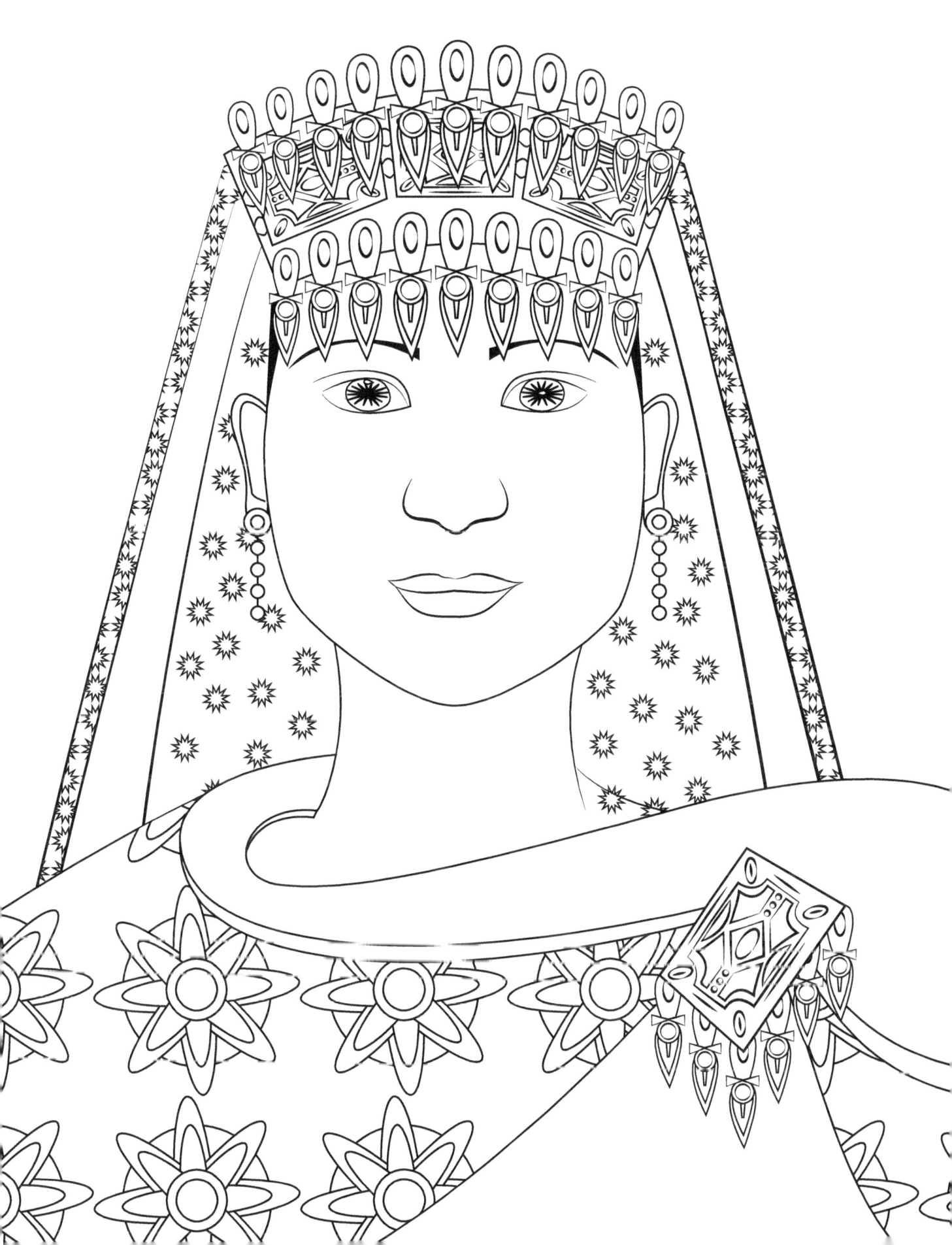

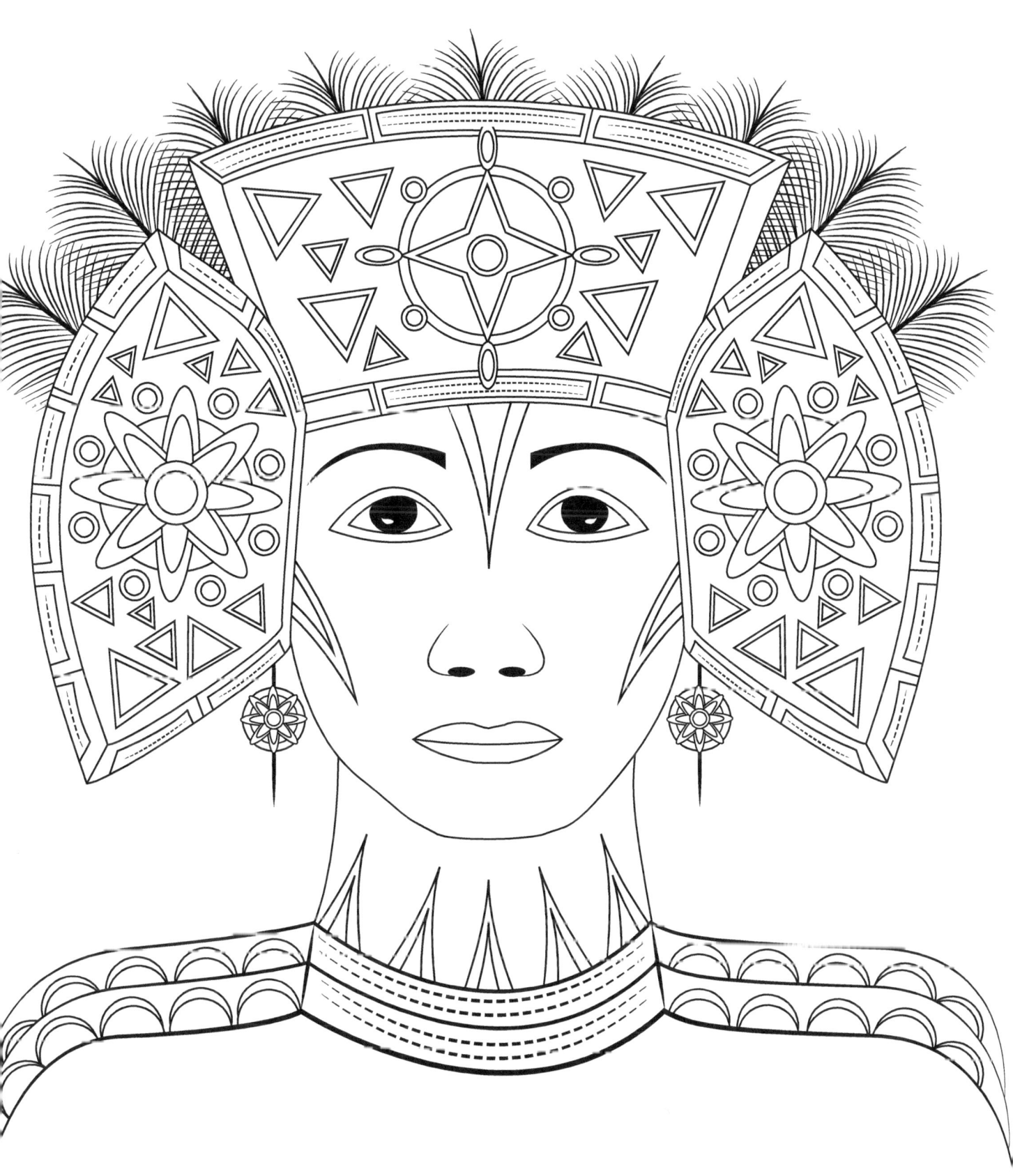

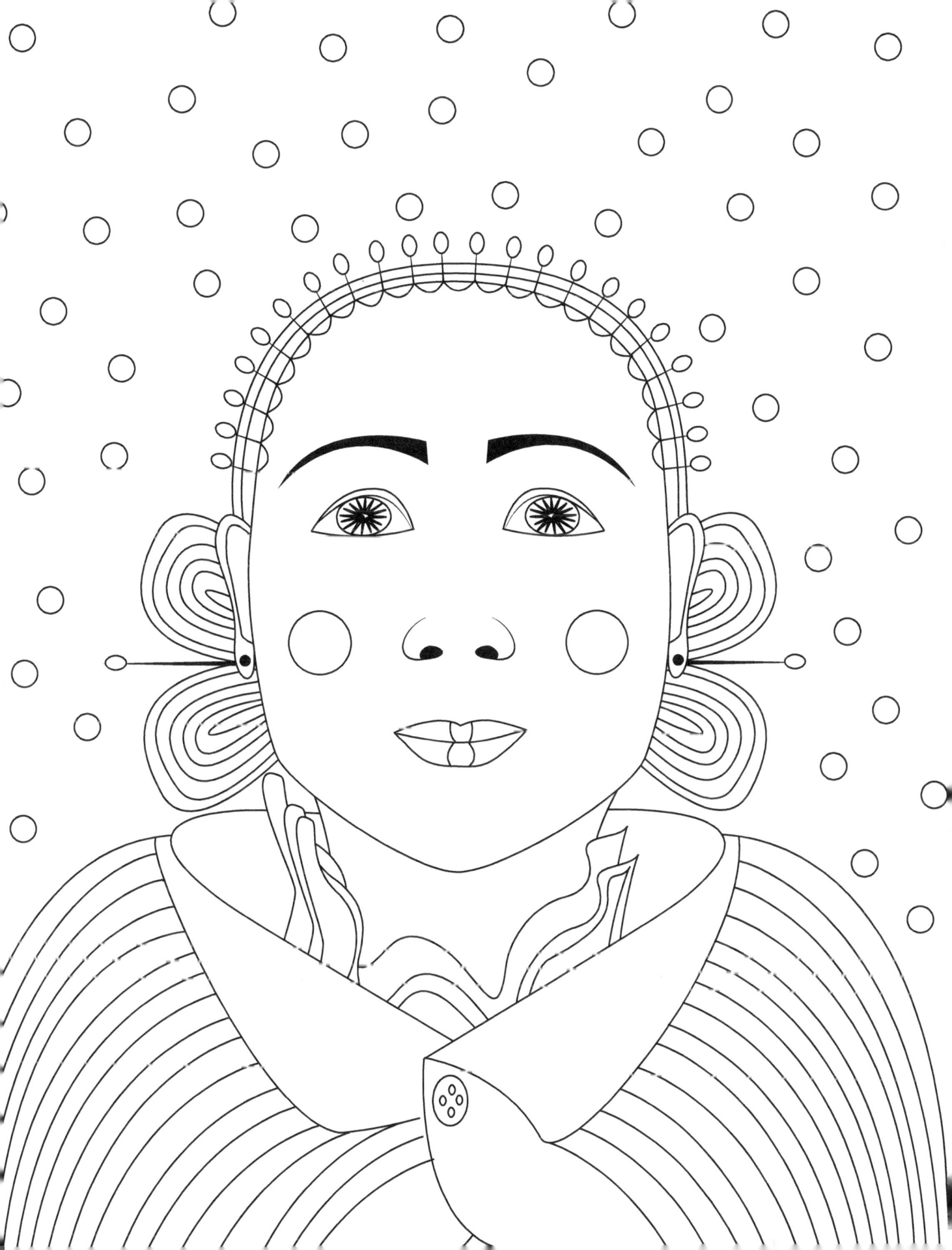

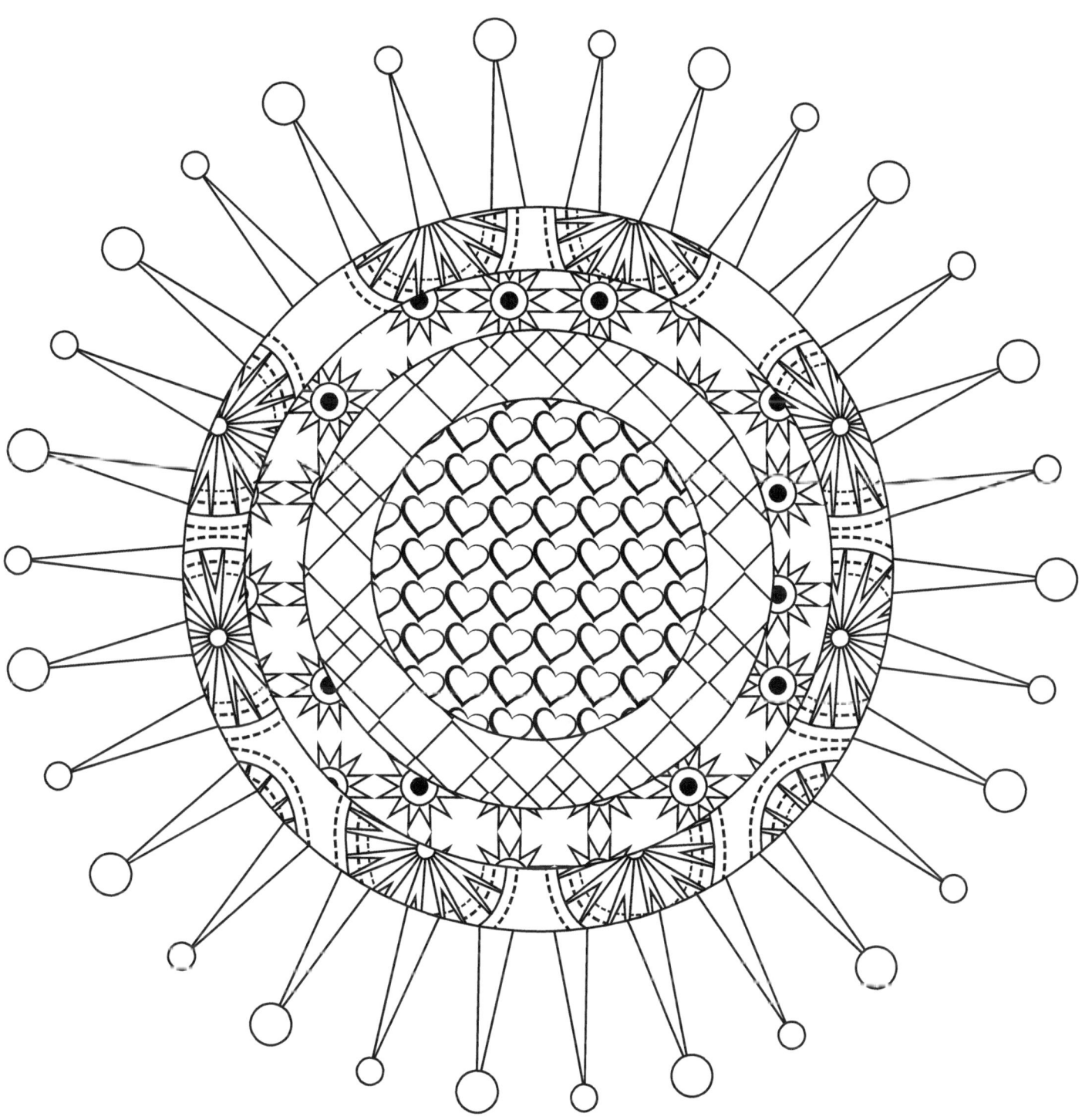

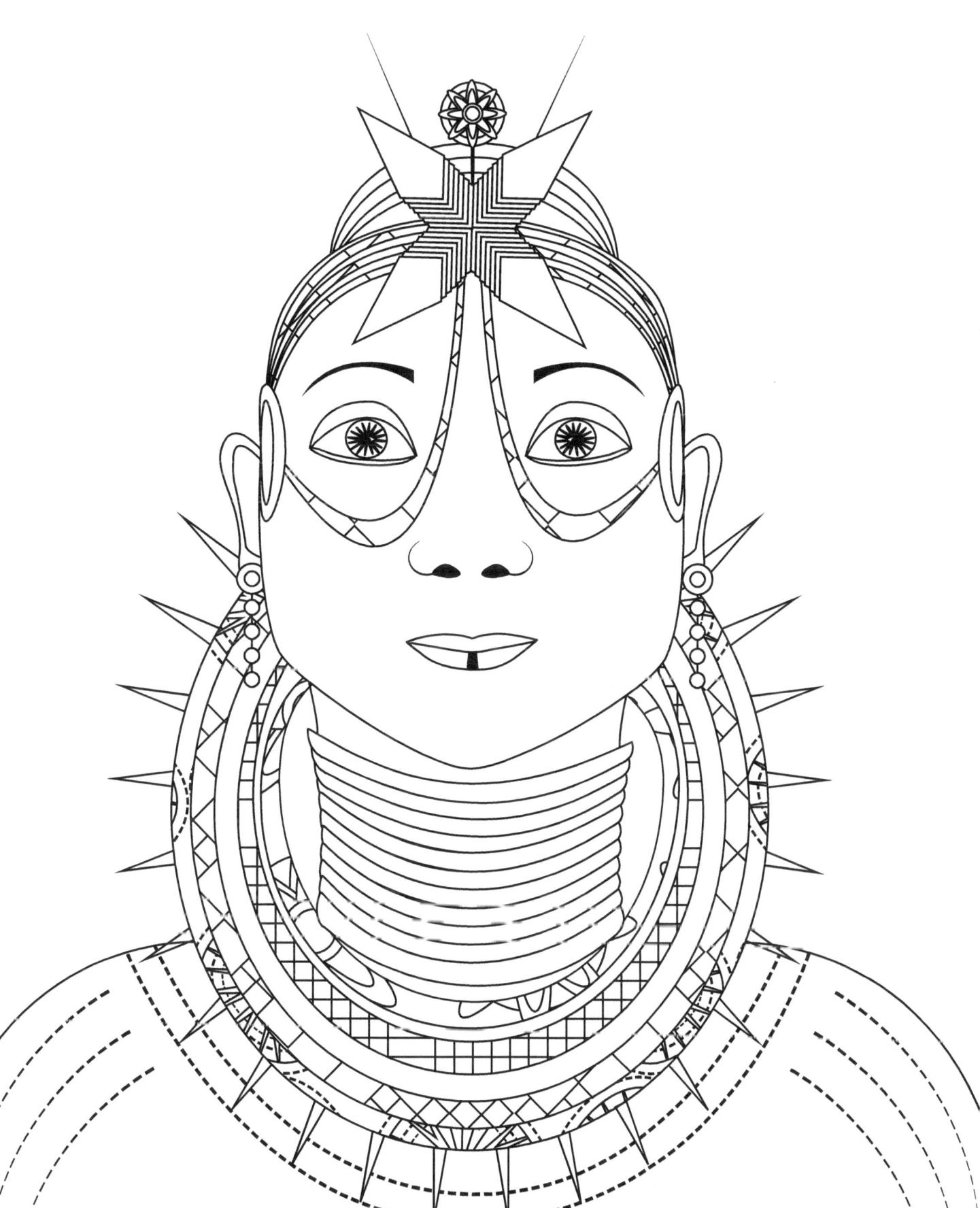

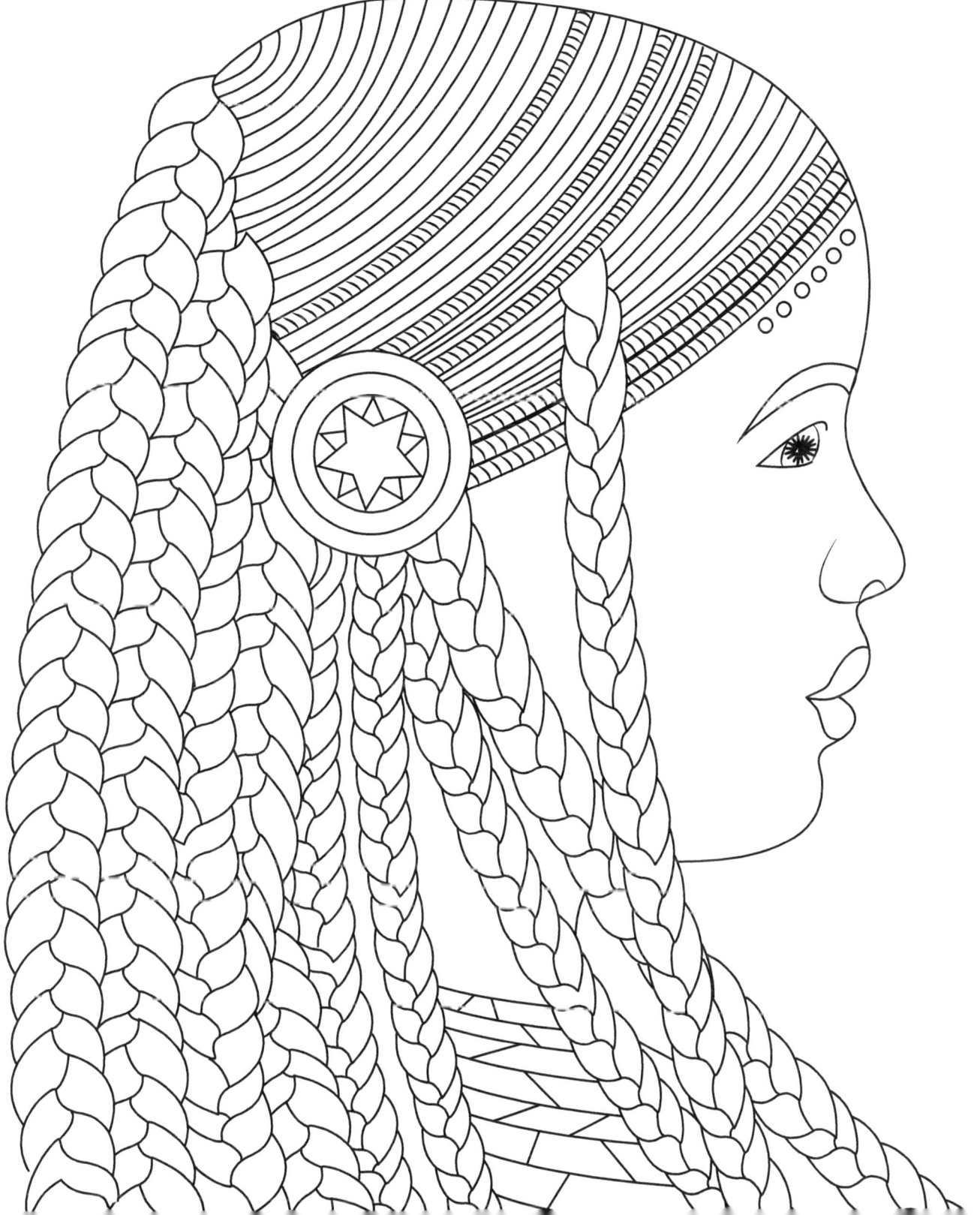

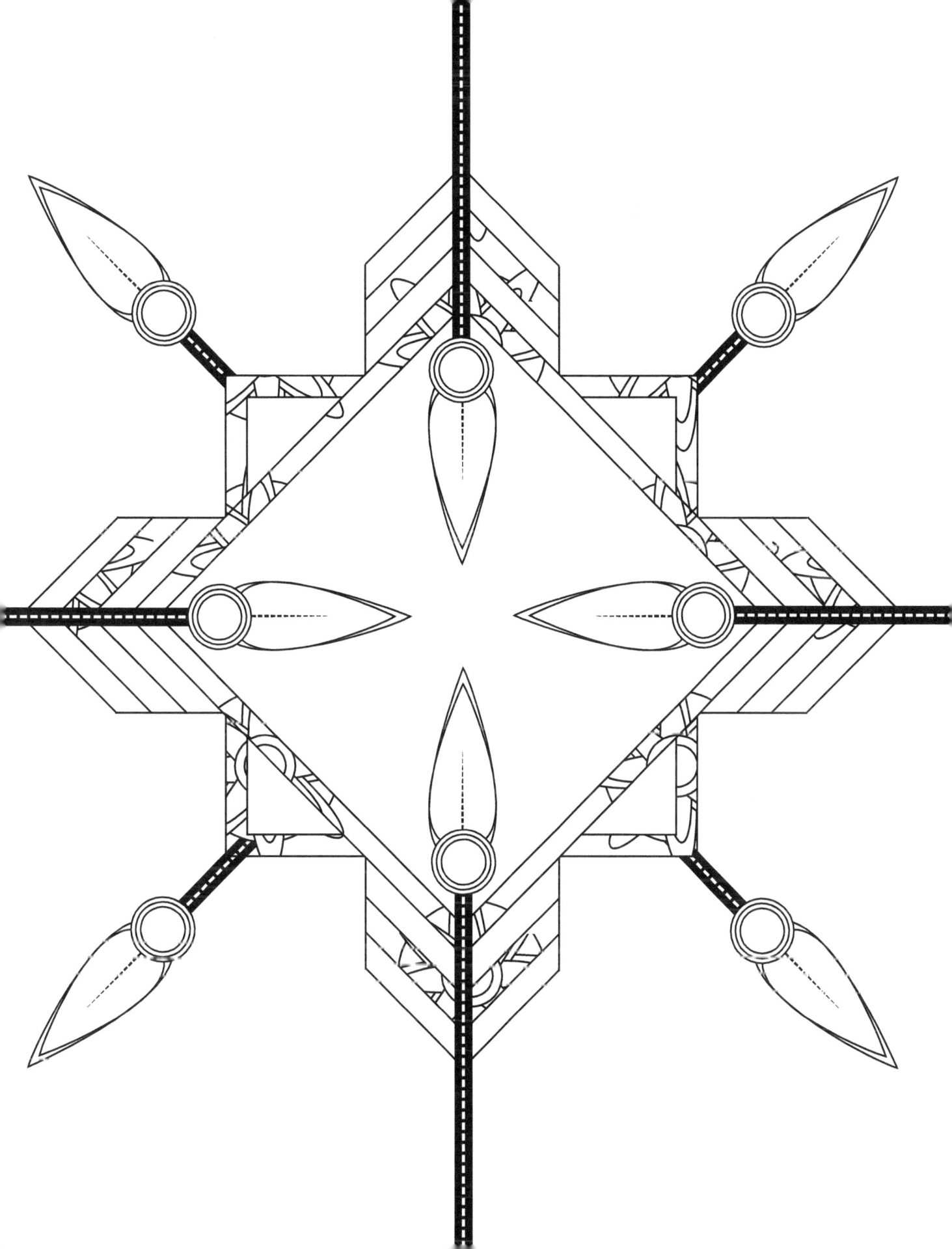

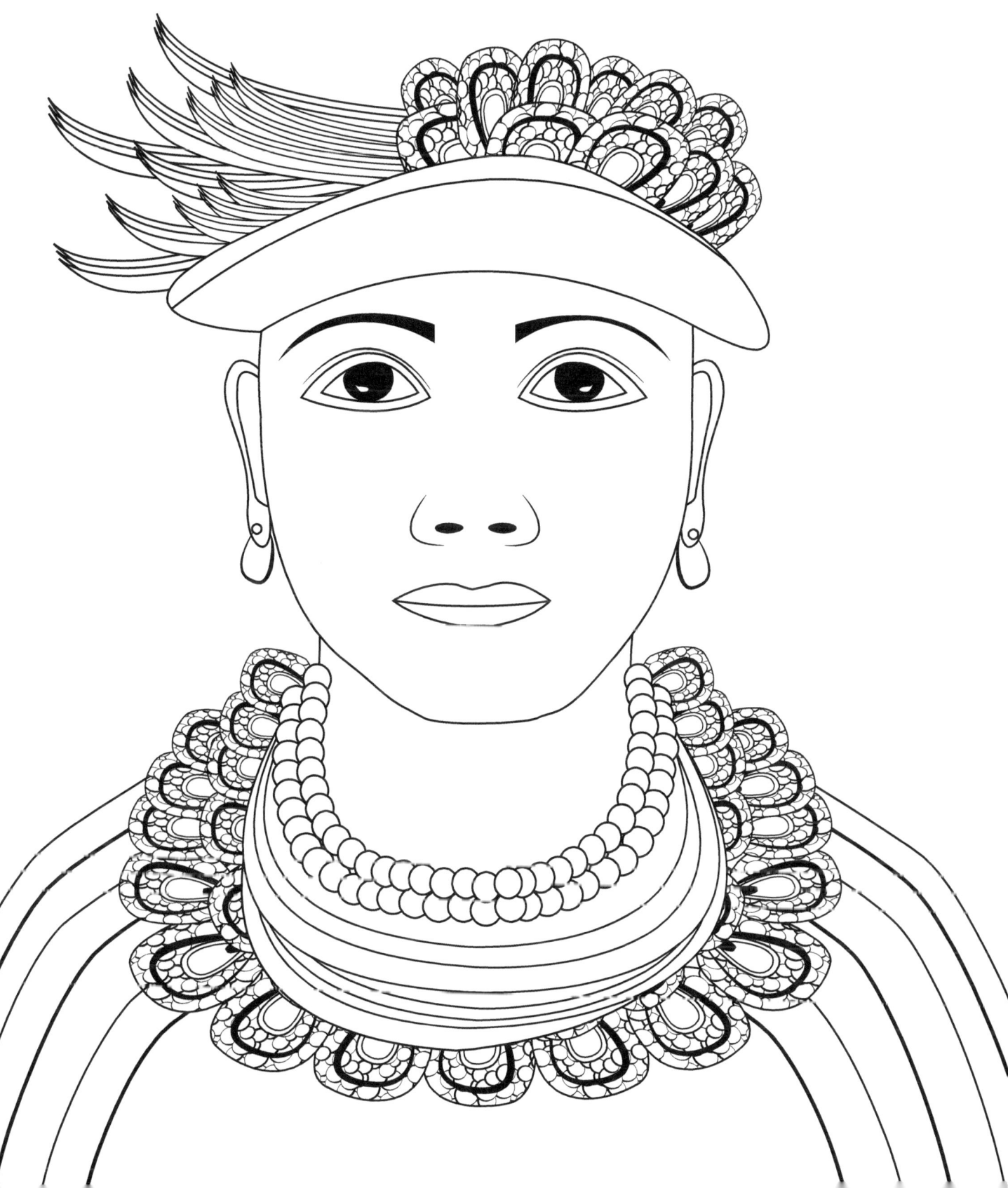

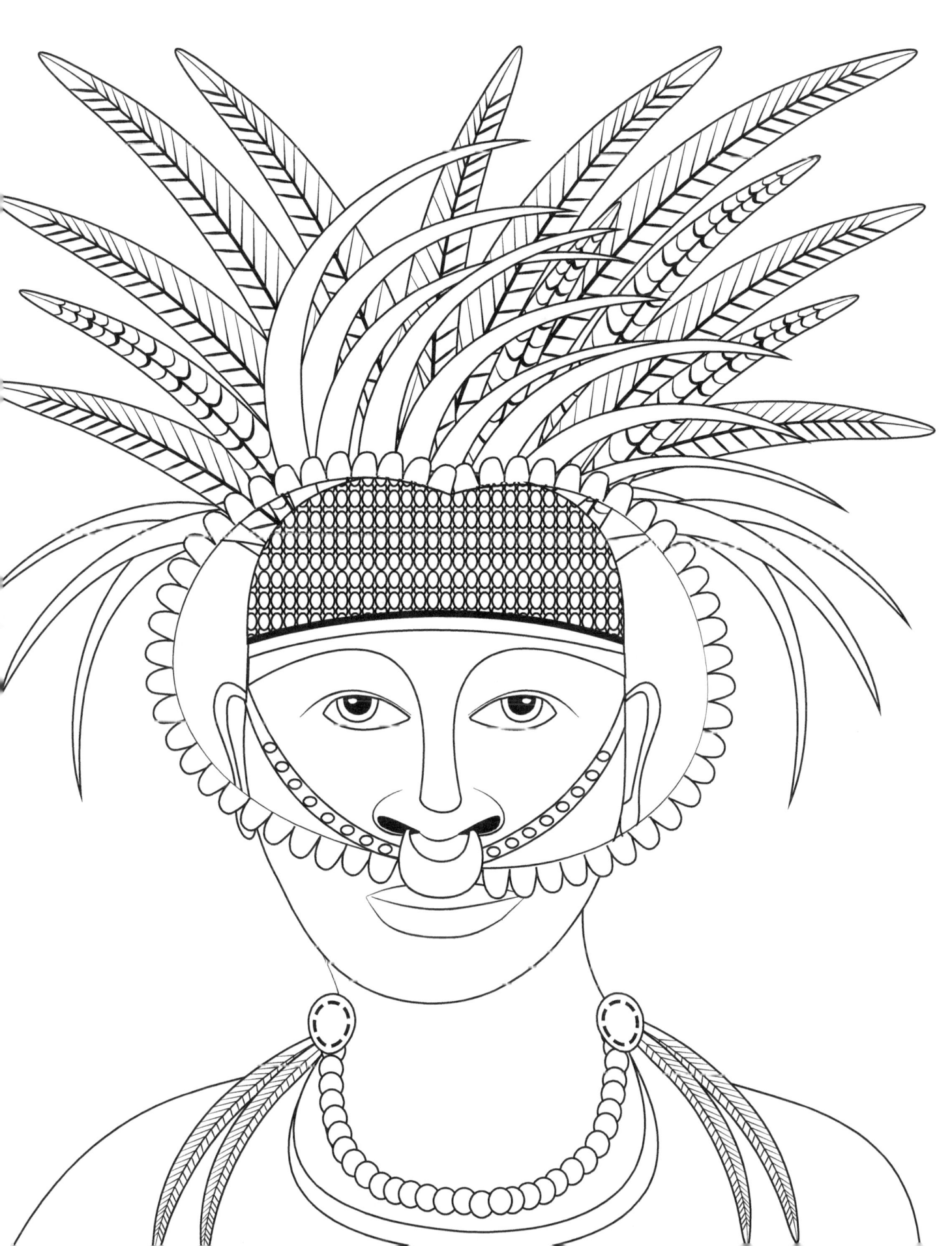

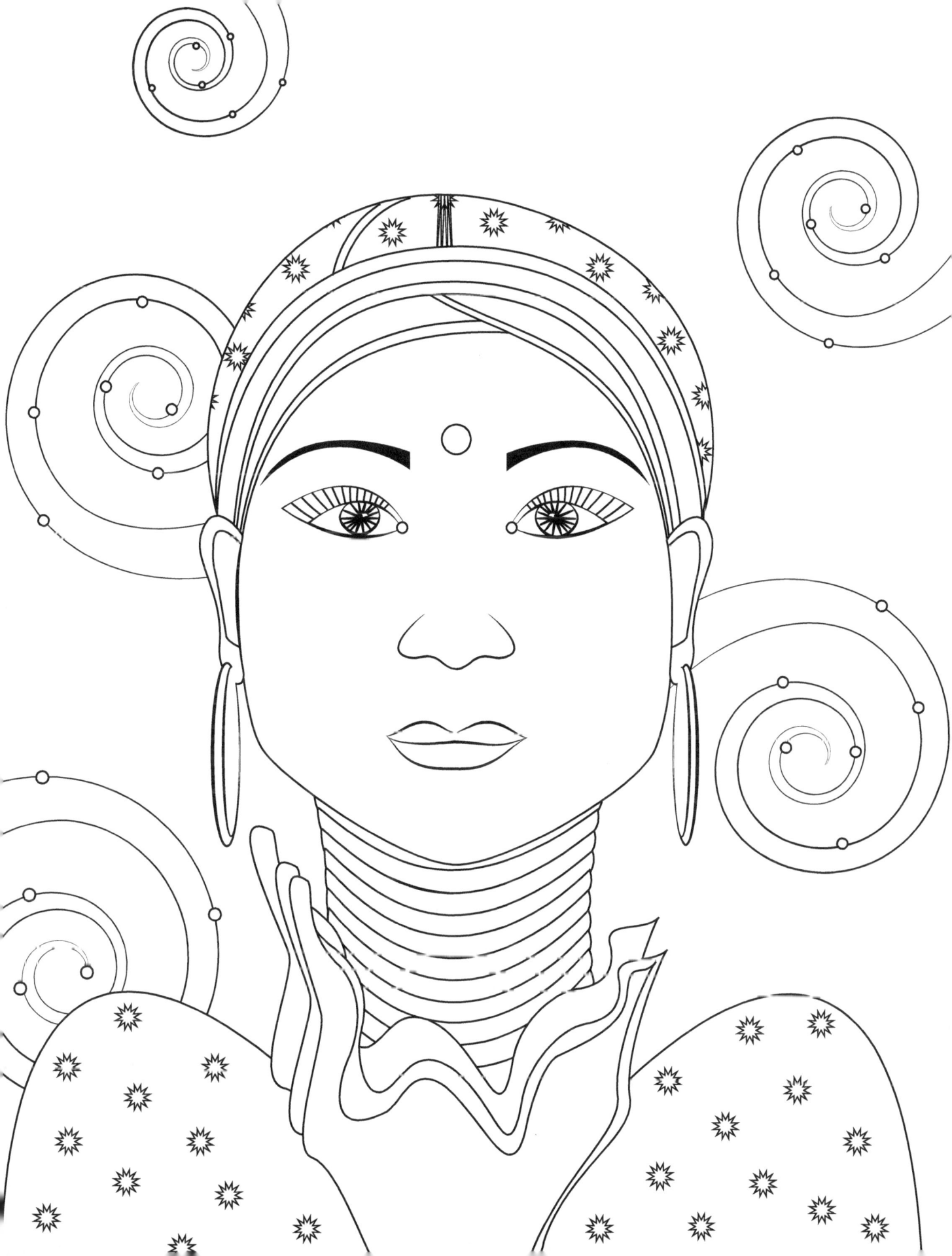

www.ingramcontent.com/pod-product-compliance
Lightning Source LLC
Chambersburg PA
CBHW081119180526
45170CB00008B/2917